CONFUCIUS IN THE BOARDROOM

Ancient Wisdom, Modern Lessons for Business

Compiled and Adapted by
Stefan Rudnicki

DOVE
B O O K S

ISBN 0-7871-1417-0

Printed in the United States of America

Dove Books
8955 Beverly Boulevard
Los Angeles, CA 90048
(310) 786-1600

Join Dove on the World Wide Web at: www.doveaudio.com/dove/

Cover Design by Peter Davis and Rick Penn-Kraus
Text design by Michele Lanci-Altomare
Layout by Rochelle Phister

First Printing: February 1998

10 9 8 7 6 5 4 3 2 1

Introduction

The Creative fosters absolute success.
Perseverence brings advancement.
—*I Ching*

The sages and philosophers of ancient China did not, as a rule, practice their profession in isolation. They were frequently engaged in political, military, or administrative activities, and they sought patronage, position, power—even property at appropriate and propitious times. In short, they behaved as businessmen. To behave otherwise would have been to deny a fundamental element of Chinese tradition—the belief in the interdependency of all actions, events, and beings.

The cover of this volume displays an emblem comprising six straight horizontal lines arranged vertically one above the other. These lines represent the first of the cycle of sixty-four hexagrams of the *I Ching*, or *Book of Changes*, an anonymous text more ancient than Confucius. The *I Ching*, with a set of commentaries written by Confucius himself, has gained popularity in this century as a divination tool, particularly after being introduced to the West through the agency of Carl Jung. The hexagram in question is named *Ch'ien, The Creative*, and serves as a perfect model for Chinese cosmology in action. Above is the trigram (three straight lines) meaning Creativity or Heaven or the Deity. Below it, as if in a mirror, rests the same trigram, symbolizing the pervasive power of Heaven in earthbound or mundane matters. "As it is above, so it is below" is the thought conveyed by this symbol, and the ultimate message is *Success*.

———

Everything has its place. Heaven is above, Earth is below, and mankind is somewhere in between. But since all derives from Heaven, its influence must be felt, accepted, and acknowledged. In this process, Man's role is perceived as that of an interpreter—a trader or dealer perhaps—who categorizes, names, and values all other things. It is the responsibility of the enlightened man to deal truly and according to his nature. But most of all, it is his responsibility to *deal*. For a sage, the most enlightened being of all, to shirk that responsibility is unthinkable. Without his involvement as arbiter and intermediary, the harmony of all beings is in jeopardy.

It is the assumption of harmony as a natural state that most identifies and unites the passages collected in this volume. Whether the source is the mystic Chuang Tzu, the militarist Sun Tzu, or the conservative pragmatist Han Fei Tzu, the one element that remains consistent is harmony: the spirit of unity in diversity and the overwhelming necessity for all beings to play the parts they are handed.

These passages serve as meditations for a life of the deepest possible involvement with the structures, patterns, and movements implicit not only in the affairs of men but also in the cycles of nature and the cosmos. As models for business, they are unparalleled.

Stefan Rudnicki
Los Angeles, 1997

CONTENTS

Chapter One

GENERAL WORLDVIEW

CH'EN TZU-ANG

BUSINESS MEN

Business men boast of skill and cunning,
But in philosophy they are like little children.
Bragging to each other of successful depredations,
They neglect to consider the ultimate fate of the body.
What should they know of the Master of Dark Truth
Who saw the wide world in a jade cup,
By illumined conception got clear of Heaven and Earth,
And on the chariot of Change entered the Gate of Immutability.

CONFUCIUS

DOCTRINE OF THE MEAN

An introduction to the principles of moderation, centrality, harmony, and equilibrium in all things—otherwise known as the Way, or Tao.

What Heaven has conferred is called NATURE.

Accordance with this Nature is called THE WAY.

Regulation of this Way is called EDUCATION.

The Way may not be left for an instant. If it could be left, it would not be the Way.

Thus, the superior man does not wait until he sees things to be cautious.

Nor does he wait until he hears things to be apprehensive.

There is nothing more visible than what is secret, and nothing more manifest than what is minute.

Therefore the superior man is watchful over himself, even when he is alone.

When there are no stirrings of pleasure, anger, sorrow, or joy, the mind may be said to be in the state of EQUILIBRIUM.

When those feelings have been stirred, and they act in their appropriate degree, there follows what may be called the state of HARMONY.

Equilibrium is the great root from which grow all the human actions in the world, and this Harmony is the universal Way which they all should pursue.

Let the states of Equilibrium and Harmony exist in perfection, and happy order will prevail throughout Heaven and Earth, and all things will be nourished and flourish.

ANALECTS

Thoughts on virtue and diversity in everyday life.

The Master said:

"Is virtue a remote thing?

"I wish to be virtuous, and look!

"Virtue is at hand."

———

Some people may work side by side, and yet disagree when they come to the logic of things. Others may agree on the logic but be wide apart in the standards they apply to it. Others still may reach the same standard together, yet be diverse in weight of character.

LAO TZU

TAO TE CHING

Defining the undefined, and understanding the Way.

Before Heaven and Earth,

Undefined, yet complete,

Formless,

Standing alone, unchanging,

Reaching everywhere.

It is the mother of all things.
I do not know its name.
I call it the Way.
Upon further reflection, I name it the Great.
Because it is great, it is in constant flow.
Passing on, it becomes distant.
Then it returns.
Therefore, the Way is great.
Heaven is great.
Earth is great.
The King is also great.
There are four great powers in the universe.
The King is one of them.
Man takes his law from the Earth
Earth takes its law from Heaven.
Heaven takes its law from the Way.
The law of the Way is to be what it is.

The paradox of opposites.

Before taking a breath, one must first release a breath.
That which weakens must first be strengthened.
To be overthrown, a thing must first be raised up.
Before anything is taken, gifts must first be given.
This is called "hiding the light."
The soft overcomes the hard; and the weak defeats
    the strong.
Fish should not be taken from the deep, and one's
    weapons should not be displayed.

LIEH-TZU

HEAVEN'S GIFTS

On the origin of all things.

Formerly the sages reduced Heaven and Earth to a system of yin and yang. But if all that has shape was born from the Shapeless, from what were Heaven and Earth born?

I answer: There was Primal Simplicity, Primal Commencement, Primal Beginnings, and Primal Material.

Primal Simplicity preceded the appearance of the breath.

Primal Commencement was the beginning of the breath.

Primal Beginnings were the breath beginning to assume shape.

Primal Material was the breath when it began to assume substance.

Breath, shape, and substance were then complete, but things were not yet separated from each other.

Hence there was Chaos. Chaos means that the myriad things were confused, and not yet separated from each other.

Looking, you did not see it; listening, you did not hear it; groping, you did not touch it. Hence the name Simple.

The Simple had no shape nor bounds. The Simple altered and became one, and from one became sevenfold, from sevenfold became ninefold. Becoming ninefold is the last of the alterations of the breath. Then it reverted to Unity. Unity is the beginning of the alterations of shape.

The pure and light rose to become Heaven, while the muddy and heavy fell to become Earth.

The breath which harmoniously combined both became Man.

Hence the essences contained by Heaven and Earth, and the birth and changing of the myriad things.

The diversity of functions, and the source of all things in the Prime Mover—being "That Which Does Nothing."

Heaven and Earth cannot achieve everything;

The sage is not capable of everything;

None of the myriad things can be used for everything.

For this reason—

It is the function of Heaven to beget and to shelter,

The function of Earth to shape and to support,

The function of the sage to teach and reform,

The function of each thing to perform its function.

Consequently, there are ways in which Earth excels Heaven, and ways in which each thing is more intelligent than the sage.

Why is this?

Heaven, which begets and shelters, cannot shape and support.

Earth, which shapes and supports, cannot teach and reform.

The sage who teaches and reforms cannot make things act counter to their functions.

Things with set functions cannot leave their places.

Hence the Way of Heaven and Earth must be either Yin or Yang; the teaching of the sage must be either kindness or justice; and the myriad things, whatever their functions, must be either hard or soft. All these observe their functions and cannot leave their places.

Hence there are the begotten and the Begetter of the begotten, shapes and the Shaper of shapes, sound and the Sounder of sounds, colors and the Colorer of colors, flavors and the Flavorer of flavors. What is begotten dies, but the Begetter never ends. Shape is real, but the Shaper has never existed. Sounds are heard, but the Sounder is out of earshot. Colors are visible, but the Colorer never appears. Flavors are tasted, but the Flavorer is never disclosed. All are the functions of That Which Does Nothing.

That Which Does Nothing is able to:

Make sweet or bitter, make foul or fragrant,

Shorten or lengthen, round off or square,

Kill or beget, warm or cool,

Float or sink, sound the highest or the lowest musical note,

Bring forth or submerge, blacken or yellow,

Make sweet or bitter, make foul or fragrant.

It knows nothing and is capable of nothing; yet there is nothing which it does not know, nothing of which it is incapable.

A perspective on life, death, and time.

When Lieh-tzu was eating at the roadside on a journey to Wei, he saw a skull a hundred years old. He picked a stalk of grass, pointed at it, and, turning to his disciple

Pai-feng, said, "He truly knows that we were never born and will never die. Is he miserable in his knowledge? Or are we happy in ours?"

The cycle of creation, death, and rebirth.

Within the seeds of all things there are germs. When they find water they develop in successive stages. Breeding on the bank, they grow from plankton into the plantain. When the plantain reaches dung, it becomes the crowfoot. The root of the crowfoot becomes woodlice, and the leaves become butterflies. The butterfly changes into an insect which breeds under the stove and looks as though it has shed its skin. After a thousand days this insect changes into a bird. The saliva of this bird generates a tiny creature which begets the gnat, which in turn begets the firefly. This firefly combines with an old bamboo which has not put forth shoots, which in time begets the leopard, which begets the horse, which begets Man.

Man in due course returns to the germs. All the myriad things come out of germs and go back to germs.

The Book of the Yellow Emperor says:

"When a shape stirs, it begets not a shape but a shadow.

"When a sound stirs, it begets not a sound but an echo.

"When Nothing stirs, it begets *not* nothing but something."

That which has shape is that which must come to an end. Will Heaven and Earth end? Will they end together with me? Will there ever be no more ending? I do not know.

Whatever is born reverts to being unborn, whatever has

shape reverts to being shapeless. That which is born is that which in principle must come to an end. Whatever ends cannot escape its end, just as whatever is born cannot escape birth; and to wish to live forever, and have no more of ending, is to be deluded about our lot.

The spirit is the possession of Heaven, the bones are the possession of Earth. What belongs to Heaven is pure and disperses, what belongs to Earth is dense and sticks together. When spirit parts from body, each returns to its true state. That is why ghosts are called *kuei*. *Kuei* means "one who has gone home." They have gone back to their true home.

The Yellow Emperor said:

"When my spirit goes through its door,

And my bones return to the root from which they grew,

What will remain of me?"

The four ages of Man.

From his birth to his end, Man passes through four great changes: infancy, youth, old age, death.

In infancy his energies are concentrated and his inclinations are one. He is in harmony. He cannot be harmed, and nothing can add to the virtue in him.

In youth, the energies in his blood are in turmoil and overwhelm him, desires and cares rise up and fill him. Others attack him, therefore the virtue wanes in him.

When he is old, desires and cares weaken, his body is moving toward rest. Nothing contends to get ahead of him, and although he has not reached the perfection of infancy, compared with his youth there is a great difference for the better.

When he dies, he goes to his rest, and thence rises again to his zenith.

CHUANG TZU

Relativity, in size, distance, and time, as derived from ancient mythic creatures.

In the Northern Ocean there is a fish, the name of which is Khwan. I do not know how many miles in size it is.

It changes into a bird with the name of Phang, the back of which is also some miles in extent. When this bird rouses itself and flies, its wings are like clouds all around the sky. When the sea disturbs it, it prepares to remove to the Southern Ocean. The Southern Ocean is the Pool of Heaven. When the Phang is removing to the Southern Ocean, it flaps its wings on the water for three thousand miles. Then it ascends ninety thousand miles on a whirlwind, and it rests only at the end of six months.

Similar to this is the movement of the breezes which we call the horses of the fields, of the dust which quivers in the sunbeams, and of living things as they are blown against one another by the air.

Is azure the real color of the sky? Or is it an illusion of distance and scale?

Moreover, there is the accumulation of water. If it is not great, it will not have strength to support a large boat. Upset a cup of water in a cavity, and a straw will float on it as if it were a boat. Place a cup in it, and it will stick fast. The water is shallow and the boat is large.

Likewise is it with the accumulation of wind. If it is not great, it will not have strength to support great wings. Therefore, the Phang would ascend to a height of ninety thousand miles, where there was a great mass of wind beneath it, and the accumulation of wind was sufficient. As it seemed to bear the blue sky on its back, and there was nothing to obstruct or arrest its course, it could pursue its way to the South.

A cicada and a little dove laughed at it, saying, "We make an effort and fly toward an elm or sapanwood tree; and sometimes before we reach it, we can do no more but drop to the ground. Of what use is it for this creature to rise ninety thousand miles and make for the South?"

He who goes to the grassy suburbs, returning for the third meal of the day, will have his belly as full as when he set out; he who goes to a distance of a hundred miles will have to pound his grain where he stops for the night; he who goes a thousand miles will have to carry with him provisions for three months. What should these two small creatures know about the matter?

The knowledge of that which is small does not reach to that which is great, and the experience of a few years does not reach to that of many. How do we know that it is so? The mushroom of a morning does not know the events of a month. The short-lived cicada does not know what takes place between the spring and autumn. These are instances of a short term of life. In the south of Khu there is a tree called Ming-ling, whose spring is five hundred years, and its autumn the same. In high antiquity there was one called Ta-khun, whose spring was eight thousand years, and its autumn the same. And the patriarch Phang is the one man renowned to the present day for his length of life. If all men were to wish to match him, would they not be miserable?

Relativity in consciousness: the butterfly dream.

The Penumbra spoke to the Shadow, saying, "Formerly you were walking, and now you have stopped; formerly you were sitting, and now you have risen up. How is it that you are so without stability?"

The Shadow replied, "I wait for the movements of something else to do what I do, and that something else on which I wait waits further on another to do as it does. My waiting—is it for the scales of a snake, or the wings of a cicada? How should I know why I do one thing, or do not do another?

"Formerly, I, Kwang Kau, dreamed that I was a butterfly, a butterfly flying about, feeling that it was enjoying itself. I did not know that it was I, Kau. Suddenly I awoke and was myself again, the veritable Kau. I did not know whether I had formerly been Kau dreaming that he was a butterfly, or was I now a butterfly dreaming that I was Kau? But between Kau and a butterfly there must be a difference. This is a case of what is called the Transformation of Things."

A parable concerning relativity and the grateful acceptance of diversity.

The god of the Southern Ocean was Shu, the god of the Northern Ocean was Hu, and the god of the Center was Chaos.

Shu and Hu were continually meeting in the land of Chaos, who treated them very well. They consulted together how they might repay his kindness, and they said, "Men all have seven orifices for the purpose of seeing, hearing, eating, and breathing, while this poor god alone has not one. Let us try and make them for him."

Accordingly they dug one orifice in him every day; and at the end of seven days Chaos died.

TZU SSU

THE WAY OF THE MEAN

Enlightenment as a function of perspective.

The Way of the enlightened man is widely apparent and yet hidden.

Thus ordinary men and women, ignorant though they are, can yet have some knowledge of it.

And yet, in its perfection, even a sage finds that there is something there which he does not know. Take the vast size of Heaven and Earth. Men can still find room for criticism of it. Hence, when the enlightened men speak of supreme size, it cannot be contained within the world of our experience.

Likewise, when they speak of supreme smallness, it cannot be perceived in the world of our senses.

———

As is said in the *Odes*:

"The hawk beats its way up to the height of Heaven, the fish dives down into the abyss."

That refers to things being examined from above and from below. This is the Way of the enlightened man, its early shoots coming into existence in the ordinary man and woman, but in its ultimate extent to be examined in the light of Heaven and Earth.

The practice of the Way. Virtue is impossible in isolation.

The Master said, "The Way is not far removed from men. If a man pursues a way which removes him from men, he cannot be in the Way.

"In the *Odes* there is the saying, 'When hewing an ax handle, hew an ax handle. The pattern of it is close at hand.' You grasp an ax handle to hew an ax handle, although, when you look from the ax in your hand to the block of wood, they are very different."

Therefore the right kind of ruler uses men to control men, and fidelity and mutual service cannot be outside the scope of the Way.

The treatment which you do not like for yourself, you must not hand out to others.

———

The acts of the enlightened man agree with the station in life in which he finds himself, and he is not concerned with matters outside that station. If he is a man of wealth and high position, he acts as such. If he is a poor man and low in the social scale, he acts accordingly. So also if he is among barbarians, or if he meets trouble.

In fact, there is no situation in which he is not himself.

HSUN TZU

SELF-CULTIVATION

Commitment to a path and principles.

Though the road is short, if a person does not travel on it, he will never reach his destination.

Though a matter be small, if he does not do it, it will never be accomplished.

If a man takes many days of leisure, he will not show much progress.

———

He who loves to follow the Way and carries it out is a scholar. He who has a firm purpose and treads the Way is a superior man. He who is inexhaustibly wise and illustrious in virtue is the sage.

———

A man who is without a rule for action is bewildered.

If he has a rule but does not understand it, he is timid.

If he relies upon the rule and understands it, only then is he calm.

SHAO YUNG

HISTORY

A method for evaluating leadership by means of historical perspective.

Since ancient times, in the administration of their empires, rulers have had four kinds of Mandates: Correct Mandate, Accepted Mandate, Modified Mandate, and Substituted Mandate.

Correct Mandate is completely followed.

Accepted Mandate is followed with some changes.

Modified Mandate is mostly changed but partly followed.

Substituted Mandate is changed completely.

That which is changed completely is work meant for a single generation. That which is mostly changed but partly followed is work meant for a hundred generations. That which is followed with some changes is work meant for a thousand generations. That which follows what ought to be followed and changes what ought to be changed is work meant for countless generations.

MAN

The centrality of mankind, and the need for harmony and balance.

The origin of Heaven and Earth is based on the principle of the Mean. Thus the heavenly and earthly principles never deviate from this central principle of existence, although they are engaged in constant transformation.

Man is central in the universe, and the mind is central in Man. The sun is most glorious and the moon is full when they are in the central position. Therefore, the principle of centrality is to be highly valued.

Our nature views things as they are, but our passions cause us to see things subjectively and egoistically. Our nature is impartial and enlightened, but our passions are partial and deceived.

When a man's qualities are characterized by the Mean and Harmony, the elements of strength and weakness in him will be balanced.

If yang predominates, he will be off balance toward strength, and if yin predominates, he will be off balance toward weakness.

As knowledge directed toward the nature of man increases, the knowledge directed toward things will decrease.

Man occupies the most honored position in the scheme of things because he combines in himself the principles of all species. If he honors his own position, he can make all species serve him.

The nature of all things is complete in the human species.

The spirit of Man is the same as the spirit of Heaven and Earth. Therefore, when a man deceives himself, he is deceiving Heaven and Earth. Let him beware!

Spirit, Mind, Truth, and the role of learning.

Spirit is nowhere and everywhere. The enlightened man can penetrate the minds of others because he is linked to the One. Spirit is called both the One and the Way. It is best to call it Spirit.

The mind is the Great Ultimate. The human mind should be as calm as still water. Being calm, it will be at peace. Being at peace, it will be enlightened.

In the pursuit of spiritual center, truth is essential. Perfect truth can penetrate all spirits. Without truth, the Way cannot be attained.

———

Our substance and nature come from Heaven, but learning derives from Man. Substance and nature develop from within, while learning enters into us from without.

The learning of a gentleman aims at enriching him. The rest, such as the mechanics of government and administration, is all secondary.

———

Without Truth, one cannot fully investigate the principle of Heaven.

Truth is the controlling factor in one's nature. It is beyond space and time.

———

He who acts in accordance with the principle of Heaven will have all of creation in his grasp. When the principle of Heaven is achieved, he is enriched in every way. His mind, his nature, and his destiny are enriched.

To be in accordance with the principle of Heaven is normal. To deviate from that principle is abnormal.

THE OBSERVATION OF THINGS

Examination of the principles inherent in the physical world, and a warning against delusions based upon emotional attachment.

When the mind retains its unity and is not disturbed, it can act on, and react to, all things harmoniously. Thus the mind of the gentleman is empty and undisturbed.

———

When observing things, one is not meant to view them with one's physical eyes but with one's mind. And not only with one's mind, but with the principle inherent in things.

There is nothing in the universe without its principle, nature, and destiny. These can be known only when principle has been investigated to the fullest, when nature is completely developed, and when destiny is fulfilled. The knowledge of these three is true knowledge. Even the sage cannot go beyond it. Whoever goes beyond it cannot be called a sage.

———

A mirror reflects because it does not obscure the physical form of things. But water, with its purity, does even better because it reveals the universal character of the form of things as they really are.

And the sage does still better because he reflects the universal character of the feelings of all things. The sage can do so because he views things as things view themselves; that is, not subjectively but from the viewpoint of the things themselves. Since he is able to do this, how can anything stand between him and the things around him?

———

When one can be happy or sad with things as though one were the things themselves, one's feelings may be said to have been aroused and to have acted to the proper degree.

We can understand things as they are if we do not impose ourselves upon them. The sage sends his thought out into the world and forgets himself.

To let the self be unrestrained is to give rein to passion; to give rein to passion is to be deluded; and to be deluded is to be ignorant.

To follow the natural principles of things, on the other hand, is to grasp their nature; to grasp their nature is to be in possession of spiritual power; and to possess spiritual power is to achieve enlightenment.

Chapter Two

POWER
AND
SUCCESS

CONFUCIUS

ANALECTS

On the difference between influence and reputation.

Tze-chang asked how the Master would describe an influential official.

"What, I wonder, do you mean by one who is influential?" said the Master.

"I mean," replied the disciple, "one who is sure to have a reputation throughout the country, as well as at home."

"That," said the Master, "is reputation, not influence.

"The influential man, then, if he is one who genuinely loves what is just and right, if he is a discriminator of men's words and an observer of their looks, and if he is in honors careful to place others ahead of himself, then he will certainly have influence, both throughout the country and at home.

"The man of mere reputation, on the other hand, who speciously affects philanthropy—though in his way he acts contrary to it, while yet evidently engrossed with that virtue—will certainly have reputation of some kind both in the country and at home."

Collecting information.

Tze-ch'in asked Tze-kung this question, "When our master comes to any country, he does not fail to learn all about its government. Does he ask information? Or is it given to him?"

Tze-kung answered, "Our master is benign, upright, courteous, and temperate, and in this way he gets his information. The master's mode of asking information—is it not different from that of other men?"

Power as a force for public, not private ends. The first shall be last.

Heaven and Earth are both long-enduring. The reason for this is that they do not live of, or for, themselves. This is how they are able to endure.

Therefore the sage places himself last, and yet he is found in the foremost ranks.

He treats himself as if he were foreign, and yet he is preserved.

Is it not because he lacks personal and private ends, that therefore such ends are realized?

LAO TZU

TAO TE CHING

The power of opposites.

It is better to leave a vessel unfilled, than to attempt to
carry it when it is full.

A blade that is oversharpened cannot long preserve
its sharpness.

When gold and jade fill the hall, their possessor cannot
keep them safe.

When wealth and honors are sought, this leads to
arrogance; a disaster is sure to follow.

When the work is done, to withdraw into obscurity is
the way of Heaven.

The partial becomes complete;

The crooked, straight;

The empty, full;

The worn out, new.

He whose desires are few gets them;

He whose desires are many goes astray.

Therefore the wise man holds in his embrace the one
And manifests it to all the world.

He is free from self-display, and therefore he shines;

From self-assertion, and therefore he is distinguished;

From boasting, and therefore his merit is acknowledged;

From complacency, and therefore he acquires superiority.

It is because he is free from striving that no one in the
world is able to strive with him.

The ancients say, "The partial becomes complete."
Is this an empty saying?
All real completion is comprehended under it.

The power of the receptive, and the need for balance in all qualities.

Know manhood's strength,
Yet maintain a woman's softness;
As to one channel flow the many streams,
All come to you, all beneath the sky.
Thus the constant excellence is nurtured;
The simple child again.
Know how white attracts,
Yet always keep within black's shade.
The pattern of humility displayed,
Displayed in view of all beneath the sky;
In unchanging excellence arrayed,
Return to the infinite.
Know how glory shines,
Yet keep humility.
Be the valley of all valleys,
To which men come from everywhere.
True and resourceful,
Return to earliest, unformed being.

The power of non-action, compliance, and receptivity.

The Tao in its regular course does nothing,
And so there is nothing which it does not do.

If princes and kings were able to apply this,
All things would of themselves develop in their course.
If action was still desirable,
They would express that desire by a return to form-
     less simplicity.
Without form, there can be no desire;
With no desire, there is only rest and stillness,
And all things go right of their own will.
The softest thing in the world overcomes the hardest;
That which has no substance may enter where there is
     no entry.
I know hereby what advantage belongs to non-action.
There are few in the world who understand
Teaching without words,
And working without doing.

———

What makes a country great is being like low land.
It becomes the meeting ground to which all under
     Heaven tend.
The female always overcomes the male by her stillness,
Lying low.
Thus it is that a great country,
By giving way to smaller countries,
Gains them for itself;
And a small country, by submitting to a greater country,
Can win it over.
In the one case the submission leads to gaining
     adherents,

In the other case to procuring favor.

The great nation wishes to unite men together and nourish them;

The small nation wishes to be received by, and to serve, the greater.

Each gets what it desires.

It is right and fitting for a great nation to submit.

Gentleness, economy, and deference.

I have three precious things which I prize and hold fast.

The first is gentleness;

The second is economy;

The third is daring not to take precedence of others.

With gentleness I can be bold;

With economy I can be generous;

Not taking precedence, I can become a vessel of the highest honor.

Nowadays men shun gentleness in favor of boldness;

They give up economy in favor of generosity;

They give up humility, and seek only to be foremost.

This is certain death.

Gentleness is sure to be victorious even in battle;

It is likewise the surest strength in defense.

It is the instrument Heaven uses to save and protect its possessor.

Humility and non-violence.

A good soldier is never violent.
A good fighter is never angry.
A good winner is never vengeful.
A good employer is humble.
Thus we say, "He never contends,
And therein is his might."
Thus we say, "Men's wills he bends,
So they with him unite."
Thus has it been since ancient times.

The conquering power of suppleness. The death of the firm and strong.

Man at his birth is supple and weak;
At his death, firm and strong.
So it is with all things.
Trees and plants, in their early growth, are soft
    and yielding;
At their death, dry and withered.
Thus it is that firmness and strength are the attributes
    of death;
Softness and weakness, the attributes of life.
Hence he who relies on the strength of his forces does
    not conquer;
And a tree which is strong and unbending soon invites
    the forester.
Therefore the place of what is firm and strong is below,
And that of what is soft and weak is above.

CHUANG TZU

Detachment. The parable of the fighting-cock.

Ki Hsing-tze was rearing a fighting-cock for the king.

Being asked after ten days if the bird was ready, he said, "Not yet. He is still vain and quarrelsome, and relies on his own vigor."

Being asked the same after another ten days, he said, "Not yet. He still responds to the crow and the appearance of another bird."

After ten days more, he replied, "Not yet. He is still spirited and possessed by anger."

When a fourth ten days had passed, he replied to the question, "Nearly so. Though another cock crows, it makes no change in him. To look at him, you would say he was a cock of wood. His quality is complete. No other cock will dare to meet him but will run from him."

CHOU TUN-I

SELECTIONS FROM AN INTERPRETATION OF THE *BOOK OF CHANGES*

Transformation as a way of life and business. The power of sincerity and oneness.

TRUTH (SINCERITY)

Truth is the essence of sagehood.

"Great is the heavenly principle, the Originator. All things derive their beginning from it."

It is the source of truth.

"The Way of the heavenly principle is to change and transform, so that everything achieves its correct nature and destiny."

In this way truth is established. It is pure and perfectly good.

Therefore, "The successive movement of the yin and the yang constitutes the Way. What issues from the Way is good and that which realizes it is individual nature."

Origination and development characterize the penetration of truth, and adaptation and correctness are its completion.

Great is the Changes, the source of nature and destiny!

SAGEHOOD

The state of absolute quiet and inactivity is truth.

Spirit is that which, "when acted on, immediately penetrates all things."

And the state of subtle emergence is the undifferentiated state between existence and nonexistence when activity has started but has not manifested itself in physical form.

Truth is infinitely pure and hence evident.

Spirit is responsive and hence works wonders.

And emergence is subtle and hence abstruse.

The sage is one who exists in a state of truth, spirit, and subtle emergence.

Can one become a sage through learning?

Yes.

The essential way is to attain oneness. By oneness is meant having no desire. Having no desire, one is empty while tranquil, and direct while in action. Being empty while tranquil, one becomes intelligent and hence penetrating. Being direct while active, one becomes impartial and hence all-embracing.

Being intelligent, penetrating, impartial, and all-embracing, one is almost a sage.

Chapter Three

LEADERSHIP
AND
MANAGEMENT

PO CHU-I

GOOD-BYE TO THE PEOPLE OF HANG-CHOW

Elders and officers line the returning road;
Wine and soup load the parting table.
I have not ruled you with the wisdom of Shao Kung;
What is the reason your tears should fall so fast?
My taxes were heavy, though many of the people were poor;
The farmers were hungry, for often their fields were dry.
All I did was to dam the water of the Western Lake
And help a little in a year when things were bad.

CONFUCIUS

ANALECTS

Simple rules for effective leadership.

The Master said, "To rule a country of a thousand chariots, there must be:

Reverent attention to business,

Truth,

Economy in expenditure,

Love for others,

The employment of the people at the proper seasons."

The value of trust.

Tze-kung asked a question relative to government.

In reply the Master listed three essentials: sufficient food, sufficient armament, and the people's confidence.

"But," said the disciple, "if you cannot have all three, and one has to be given up, which would you give up first?"

"The armament," he replied.

"And if you are obliged to give up one of the remaining two, which would it be?"

"The food," said the Master. "Death has been the portion of all men from of old. Without the people's trust, nothing can stand."

Rules of conduct and behavior for leaders.

Let a leader show rectitude in his own personal character, and even without directions from him things will go well. If he is not personally upright, his directions will not be complied with.

Let a ruler but see to his own rectitude, and what trouble will he then have in the work before him? If he be unable to rectify himself, how is he to rectify others?

———

There were four things from which the Master was entirely free.

He had no foregone conclusions, no arbitrary predeterminations, no obstinacy, and no egoism.

———

The Master said, "If the people are led by laws, and compliance is enforced for them by punishments, they will try to avoid the punishment, but they will have no sense of shame.

"If they are led by virtue, and compliance reinforced for them by the rules of propriety, they will have a sense of shame, and moreover they will become good."

———

The superior man undergoes three changes. Looked at from a distance, he appears stern. When approached, he is mild. When he is heard to speak, his language is firm and decided.

———

Tze-chang asked Confucius, "In what way should a person in authority act in order that he may conduct business properly?"

The Master said, "Let him honor the five excellent things, and banish the four bad things. Then he may conduct business properly."

Tze-chang asked, "What are the five excellent things?"

The Master said, "When the person in authority is beneficent without great expenditure; when he lays tasks on the people without generating complaint; when he pursues what he desires without being greedy; when he maintains a dignified ease without being proud; when he is majestic without being fierce."

Tze-chang asked, "What is meant by being beneficent without great expenditure?"

The Master replied, "When the person in authority makes more available to the people the things from which they naturally derive benefit—is not this being beneficent without great expenditure? When he chooses the labors which are proper, and makes them labor on them, who will complain? When his desires are set on benevolent government and he secures it, who will accuse him of greed? Whether he has to do with many people or few, or with things great or small, he does not dare to indicate any disrespect—is not this to maintain a dignified ease without any pride? He adjusts his clothes and cap, and throws a dignity into his looks so that, thus dignified, he is looked at with awe—is not this to be majestic without being fierce?"

Tze-chang then asked, "What is meant by the four bad things?"

The Master said, "To put people to death without having instructed them—this is called cruelty. To require from them, suddenly, the full measure of work without having given them warning—this is called oppression. To issue orders as if without urgency, at first, and when the time comes, to insist on them with severity—this is called injury. And, generally, in giving pay or rewards to men, to do it in a stingy way—this is called acting the part of a mere official."

———

The Master said, "Without recognizing the ordinances of Heaven, it is impossible to be a superior man.

"Without an acquaintance with the rules of Propriety, it is impossible for the character to be established.

"Without knowing the force of words, it is impossible to know men."

———

Confucius was asked about government.

"Lead the way in it," said the Master, "and work hard at it."

Requested to say more, he added, "And do not tire of it."

LAO TZU

TAO TE CHING

Leadership by indirection.

Not to value and employ men of superior ability is
the way to keep the people from rivalry among
themselves;

Not to prize riches is the way to prevent stealing;
Not to show what is likely to excite desires is the way
    to keep minds from disorder.
Therefore the sage, in the exercise of his leadership,
    empties their minds, fills their bellies, weakens their
    wills, and strengthens their bones.
He constantly tries to keep them without knowledge
    and without desire,
And where there are those who have knowledge, he
    tries to keep them from presuming to act on it.
Where nothing is done, good order prevails.

The leader's identification with his constituency.

The sage has no invariable mind of his own;
He makes the mind of the people his mind.
To those who are good, I am good;
And to those who are not good, I am also good;
And thus all get to be good.
To those who are faithful, I am faithful;
And to those who are not faithful, I am also faithful;
And thus all get to be faithful.
The sage has, to the world, an appearance of indecision,
And keeps his mind in a state of indifference to all.
The people all keep their eyes and ears directed to him,
And he is as a child with them.

The virtues of ignorance. Security in the workplace.

The ancients who were skilled in practicing the Tao
    did not enlighten the people,

But rather kept them ignorant.
The difficulty in governing the people arises from their
    having much knowledge.
He who tries to govern a country by his wisdom
Is a scourge to it;
While he who rules without it is a blessing.
He who knows these two things
Finds in them also his model and rule.
Ability to know this model and rule
Constitutes what we call the mysterious excellence.
Deep and far-reaching is such mysterious excellence,
Leading back to oneness.

CHUANG TZU

The enlightened leader.

Kun Mang, on his way to the ocean, met with Yuan Fung on the shore of the eastern sea, and was asked by him where he was going.

"I am going," he replied, "to the ocean."

And Yuan Fung asked, "What for?"

Kun Mang said, "Such is the nature of the ocean that the waters which flow into it can never fill it, nor those which flow from it exhaust it. I will enjoy myself, rambling by it."

Yuan Fung said, "Have you no thoughts about mankind? I should like to hear from you about sagely government."

Kun Mang said, "Under the government of sages, all offices are distributed according to the fitness of their nature; all appointments are made according to the ability of the men; whatever is done is after a complete survey of all circumstances; actions and words proceed from the inner impulse, and the whole world is transformed. Wherever their hands are pointed and their looks directed, from all quarters the people are all sure to come to do what they desire. This is what is called government by sages."

"I should like to hear about the government of kindly, virtuous men," continued Yuan Fung.

The reply was, "Under the government of the virtuous, when tranquilly occupying their place, they have no thought. When they act, they have no anxiety. They do not keep stored in their minds what is right and what is wrong, what is good and what is bad. They share their benefits among all within the four seas, and this produces what is called satisfaction. They dispense their gifts to all, and this produces what is called peace.

"The people grieve on their death like babies who have lost their mothers, and are perplexed like travelers who have lost their way. They have a superabundance of wealth and all necessaries, and they know not whence it comes. They have a sufficiency of food and drink, and they know not from whom they get it.

"Such are appearances under the government of the kindly and virtuous."

"I should like to hear about the government of spiritual men," continued Yuan Fung once more.

The reply was, "Men of the highest spiritual qualities mount up on the light, and the limitations of the body vanish. This we call being bright and ethereal. They carry out to the utmost the powers with which they are endowed, and have not a single attribute unexhausted. Their joy is that of Heaven and Earth, and all embarrassments of business melt away and disappear.

"All things return to their proper nature. And this is what is called chaotic obscurity."

A model for great leadership: the sun and moon.

Anciently, Shun spoke with Yao, saying, "In what way does your Majesty, by the Grace of Heaven, exercise your mind?"

The reply was, "I simply show no arrogance toward the helpless. I do not neglect poor people. I grieve for those who die. I love their infant children, and I am compassionate toward their widows."

Shun rejoined, "Admirable, as far as it goes. But it is not what is Great."

"How then," asked Yao, "do you think I should behave?"

Shun replied, "If a sovereign possesses the virtue of Heaven, then when he shows himself in action, it is in stillness. The sun and moon simply shine, and the four seasons pursue their courses. So it is with the regular phenomena of day and night, and with the movement of the clouds by which the rain is distributed."

Yao said, "Then I have only been persistently troubling myself! What you recommend is to be in harmony with Heaven, while I have been merely in harmony with men."

Now the Way of Heaven and Earth was much thought of in olden times, and Hwang-Ti, Yao, and Shun united in admiring it. Hence the kings of the world of old did nothing, but tried to imitate that Way.

HAN FEI TZU

SIX CONTRARIETIES

A repudiation of Confucian and Taoist non-action by the precursor of imperialism and aggressive capitalism. To be attempted only if all other methods fail.

The ancients had a proverb saying: "To govern the people is like washing one's head. Though there are falling hairs, the washing must be done."

Whoever laments the waste of falling hairs and forgets the gain of the growing hairs does not know the doctrine of expediency.

Opening boils causes pain, and taking drugs produces a bitter taste. Yet, if boils are not opened on account of pain, and drugs not taken on account of bitterness, the person will not live and the disease will not stop.

The learned men of today, on counseling the lord of men, all persuade him to discard the profit-seeking mind and follow the way of mutual love. Thereby they demand more from the lord of men than from parents. Such is an immature view of human relationships; it is both deceitful and fallacious. Naturally the enlightened sovereign would not accept it.

The sage, in governing the people, deliberates upon laws and prohibitions. When laws and prohibitions are clear and manifest, all officials will be in good order. He makes reward and punishment definite. When reward and punishment are never unjust, the people will attend to public duties. If the people attend to public duties and officials are in good order, then the state will become rich. If the state is rich, then the army will become strong. In consequence, empire will be attained.

The enterprise of the Emperor is the highest goal of the lord of men. With this highest goal in view, the lord of men attends to business. Therefore, the officials he appoints to office must have the required abilities, and the rewards and punishments he enforces must involve no selfishness, but manifest public justice to gentry and commoners alike.

Whoever exerts his strength and risks his life will be able to accomplish merits and attain rank and bounty. When rank and bounty have been attained, the enterprise of wealth and nobility will be accomplished.

Now, wealth and nobility constitute the highest goal of the ministers. With this highest goal in view, the ministers attend to their official duties. Therefore, they will work hard, even at the peril of their lives, and never resent the exhaustion of their energy.

This amounts to the saying that if the ruler is not benevolent and the ministers are not loyal, empire cannot be attained.

Indeed, liberal rewards are meant not only to reward men of merit but also to encourage the whole state. The rewarded enjoy the benefits; those not as yet rewarded look forward to their future accomplishment. This is to requite one man for his merit and to encourage the whole populace within the boundaries. Therefore, why should those who want order doubt the efficacy of liberal rewards?

TUNG CHUNG-SHU

LUXURIANT GEMS OF THE SPRING AND AUTUMN ANNALS

The foundation of leadership in harmony with Heaven and Earth. Spontaneous punishment and reward.

The ruler is the foundation of the state.

In administering the state, nothing is more effective for educating the people than reverence for this foundation.

If this foundation is revered, then the ruler may transform the people as though by supernatural power.

But if the foundation is not revered, then the ruler will have nothing by which to lead his people. Then, though he employs harsh penalties and severe punishments, the people will not follow him. This will drive the state to ruin, and there is no greater disaster.

What do we mean by this foundation?

Heaven, Earth, and Man are the foundation of all creatures. Heaven gives them birth, Earth nourishes them, and Man brings them to completion.

Heaven provides them at birth with a sense of filial and brotherly love.

Earth nourishes them with clothing and food.

Man completes them with rites and music.

The three act together as hands and feet join to complete the body, and none can be dispensed with.

If all three are lacking, then the people will become like deer, each person following his own desires, each family possessing its own ways. Fathers cannot employ their sons nor rulers their ministers, and though there be walls and battlements, they will be called an empty city.

Then will the ruler lie down with a clod of earth for a pillow. Although no one is menacing him, he will endanger himself. Although no one is destroying him, he will destroy himself.

This is called a spontaneous punishment, and when it descends, though he hides in halls of encircling stone or barricades himself behind steep defiles, he can never escape.

But the enlightened and worthy ruler, being of good faith, is strictly attentive to the three foundations. His sacrifices are conducted with utmost reverence. He serves and makes offerings to his ancestors. He advances brotherly affection and encourages filial conduct.

In this way he serves the foundation of Heaven.

He personally grasps the plow handle and plows a furrow, plucks the mulberry himself and feeds the silkworms, breaks new ground to increase the grain supply and opens the way for a sufficiency of clothing and food. In this way he serves the foundation of Earth.

He sets up schools for the nobles and in the towns and villages, to teach filial piety and brotherly affection, reverence and humility. He enlightens the people with education and moves them with rites and music. Thus he serves the foundation of Man.

If he rightly serves these three, then the people will be like sons and brothers, not daring to be unsubmissive. They will regard their country as a father or a mother, not waiting for favors to love it, not for coercion to serve it. And even if they dwell in fields and camp beneath the sky, they will count themselves more fortunate than if they lived in palaces.

Then will the ruler rest on a secure pillow.

Though none aid him, he will grow mighty of himself.

Though none pacify his kingdom, peace will come of its own.

This is called a spontaneous reward, and when it comes, though he relinquish his throne, give up his kingdom, and depart, the people will take up their children on their backs, follow him, and keep him as their lord, so that he can never leave them.

The importance of humanity. How the leader's passions parallel the weather and seasonal changes, and his concomitant responsibility.

Those who, in ancient times, invented writing, drew

three lines and connected them through the middle, calling the character "king."

The three lines which comprise this character are Heaven, Earth, and Man, and the line which passes through the middle joins the principles of all three. Occupying the center of Heaven, Earth, and Man, passing through and joining all three—if this is not a king, what is?

Thus the king is but the executor of Heaven. He regulates its seasons and brings them to completion. He patterns his actions on its commands and causes the people to follow them.

When he would begin some enterprise, he observes its numerical laws. He follows its ways in creating his laws, observes its will, and brings all to rest in humanity.

The highest humanity rests with Heaven, for Heaven is humaneness itself.

It shelters and sustains all creatures.

It transforms them and brings them to birth.

It nourishes and completes them.

Its works never cease. They end and then begin again, and the fruits of its labors it gives to the service of mankind. He who looks into the will of Heaven must perceive its endless and inexhaustible humaneness.

Since Man receives his life from Heaven, he must also take from Heaven its humaneness and himself be humane. Therefore he reveres Heaven and knows the affections of father and son, brother and brother.

He has a heart of trust and faithfulness, compassion and mercy.

He is capable of acts of decorum and righteousness, modesty and humility.

He can judge between right and wrong, between what accords with and what violates duty.

His sense of moral order is brilliant and deep, and his understanding is great, encompassing all things.

Only the way of Man can form a triad with Heaven.

Heaven's will is constantly to love and benefit, its business to nourish and bring to maturity. Spring and autumn, winter and summer are all instruments of its will.

The will of the king likewise is to love and benefit the world. His business is to bring peace and joy to his time. His love and hate, his joy and anger, are his instruments. The loves and hates, joys and angers of the king are no more than the spring and summer, autumn and winter, of Heaven.

It is by the changes of weather—mild or cool, hot or cold—that all things are transformed and brought to fruition. If Heaven puts these forth in the proper season, then the year will be a ripe one. But if the weather is unseasonable, the year will be lean.

In the same way, if the ruler of men exercises his love and hate, his joy and anger, in accordance with righteousness, then the age will be well governed. But if he does so unrighteously, then the age will be in confusion.

Thus we know that the art of governing well and bringing about a ripe year are the same; that the principle behind a chaotic age and a lean year is identical. So we see that the principles of mankind correspond to the way of Heaven.

The cool and mild, the cold and hot seasons of Heaven are actually one and the same with Man's emotions of contentment and anger, sorrow and joy. These four temperaments are shared by Heaven and Man alike, and are not something engendered by Man alone.

Therefore Man can regulate his emotions, but he cannot extinguish them. If he regulates them, they will follow with what is right, but if he attempts to suppress them, disorder will result.

The spirit of spring is loving. The spirit of autumn is stern. The spirit of summer is joyous, and that of winter is sad.

Therefore the breath of spring is mild, for Heaven is loving and begets life. The breath of summer is warm, and Heaven makes glad and nourishes. The breath of autumn is cool, and so Heaven is stern and brings all to fruition. The breath of winter is cold, and Heaven grieves and lays all to rest.

Spring presides over birth, summer over growth, autumn over the gathering in, and winter over the storing away.

The ruler holds the position of life and death over men.

Together with Heaven he holds the power of change and transformation.

There is no creature that does not respond to the changes of Heaven. The changes of Heaven and Earth are like the four seasons. When the wind of their love blows, then the air will be mild and the world will teem with life. But when the winds of their disfavor come forth, the air will be cold and all things die. When they are joyous, the skies are warm and all things grow and flourish, but from their wrath comes the chill wind and all is frozen and shut up.

The ruler of men uses his love and hate, his joy and anger to change and reform the customs of men, as Heaven employs warm and cool, cold and hot weather to transform the grass and trees. If joy and anger are seasonably applied, then the year will be prosperous, but if they are used wrongly and out of season, the year will fail.

Heaven, Earth, and Man are one, and therefore the passions of Man are one with the seasons of Heaven. So the time and place for each must be considered. If Heaven produces heat in the time for cold, or cold in the season of heat, then the year must be unfruitful. So also, if the ruler manifests anger when joy would be appropriate, or joy where anger is needed, then the age must fall into chaos.

Therefore the great concern of the ruler lies in diligently watching over his heart, that his loves and hates, his angers and joys may be displayed in accordance with right, as the mild and cool, the cold and hot weather come forth in proper season.

If the ruler constantly practices this without error, then his emotions will never be at fault, as spring and autumn, winter and summer are never out of order. Then may he form a trinity with Heaven and Earth.

If he holds these four passions deep within him and does not allow them recklessly to come forth, then may he be called the equal of Heaven.

KUO HSIANG

SELF-TRANSFORMATION AND TAKING NO ACTION

Discreet and individual functions.

In the cutting of a tree, the workman does not take any action; the only action he takes is in plying the ax.

In the actual managing of business, the ruler does not take any action; the only action he takes is in employing his ministers.

If the ministers can manage affairs, the ruler employ ministers, the ax cut the tree, and the workman use the ax—each corresponding to his capacity—then the laws of nature will operate of themselves, and not because someone takes action.

If the ruler does the work of his ministers, he will no longer be the ruler, and if the ministers control the ruler, they will no longer be ministers. Therefore when each attends to his own responsibility, both ruler and ruled will be contented and the principle of taking no action will be attained.

An alternate explanation of non-action, based on the importance of influence and interdependence. The story of Yao and Hsu-yu.

Only he who does no governing can govern the empire.

Therefore Yao governed by not governing. It was not because of his governing that his empire was governed.

Now the recluse Hsu-yu only realized that since the empire was well-governed he should not replace Yao. He thought it was Yao who did the actual governing. Consequently he said to Yao: "You govern the empire."

Someone may say, "It was Yao who actually governed and put the empire in good order, but it was Hsu-yu who enabled Yao to do so by refusing to govern himself."

This is a great mistake. Yao was an adequate example of governing by not governing and acting by not acting. Why should we have to resort to Hsu-yu? Are we to insist that a man fold his arms and sit in silence in the middle of some mountain forest before we will say he is practicing "non-action"? This is why the words of Lao Tzu and Chuang Tzu are rejected by responsible officials. This is why responsible officials insist on remaining in the realm of action without feeling any regret.

By taking no action is not meant folding one's arms and closing one's mouth. If we simply let everything act by itself, it will be contented with its nature and destiny. To have no alternative but to rule an empire is not to be forced into doing so by power or punishment. If only the Way is embraced and simplicity cherished, and what has to be is allowed to run its maximum course, then the world will naturally be contented with itself.

HUANG TSUNG-HSI

KINGSHIP

A theory of the rise of authority in human affairs.

In ancient times, every man labored for himself and for his private interests, and there was no one to think of the public good or fight a common evil of society.

Then the kings arose who worked for the public good and not the good of their own selves. They fought what was evil to the community as a whole and neglected what might be good for their own selves.

Thus kings were people who worked a thousand times harder than the people, without benefit to themselves. This was hardly an enviable position.

Therefore, there were those who worked for the public benefit and never wanted to be called kings, like Shuyu and Wukuang.

And there were other rulers who worked for the public benefit as kings, and then handed over their power to others, like Yao and Hsun.

And there were yet others who were made kings and were forced to remain kings, like Yu.

It was human nature, whether ancient or modern, not to relish such a position.

***Power corrupts. Professional leadership. A plea for account-
ability in leadership.***

The kings of later times were different.

They concentrated the power of government in themselves, and having done so, thought it allowable to take all
the profits of the land for themselves and throw all that was
disagreeable and onerous upon others, so that the people
were not able to work for their own benefit or their own
good, while the profits of the land became the private
property of one family.

At first, the kings felt embarrassed, but later they lost
such embarrassment. The land and the people then
belonged to one ruling house, the exclusive right and priv-
ilege to be handed down to their children and their children's children.

The First Emperor of Han betrayed this way of think-
ing when he said to a scholar, "Do you think my success at
my profession is greater or lesser than yours?" To him,
being a king was a profession, like all others carried on for
personal benefit.

The difference lies in this: In ancient times, the people
were the masters, and the kings the guests; and the object
of the kings' labors was the people. Now it is the kings who
are the masters and the people the guests, and there is not
one corner of the earth where the people can live peace-
fully their own lives, all because of the rulers.

Therefore when someone aspires to be a king, he does
not mind sacrificing the lives of millions and taking away

children from their parents in order to work for his private advantage.

Without the slightest qualm of conscience, he says, "I am building up this ruling house for my children." And when he has attained to kingship, he does not mind grinding out the bones and marrow of the people and breaking up families to labor and service, that he alone may enjoy all the luxury and amusements of easy living.

Without a qualm of conscience, he says again to himself, "I am entitled to the earnings of my property, am I not?"

Kings have thus become the great enemy of the people. For if there were no kings, people would be able to work for their own benefit and their own living. Alas! is this the purpose for which kings exist?

Chapter Four

PLANNING, TIMING, AND CYCLES

CONFUCIUS

ANALECTS

Effective time.

"Were any of our princes to employ me," the Master said, "after a twelvemonth I might have made some tolerable progress. But give me three years, and my work should be done."

LAO TZU

TAO TE CHING

Anticipation in all things.

Peace is easily kept hold of;
Before trouble has given indications of its presence,
It is easy to take measures against it;
That which is brittle is easily broken;
That which is very small is easily dispersed.
Action should be taken before a thing has made its
*   appearance;*
Order should be secured before disorder has begun.
The tree thick enough to fill a man's arms grows from
*   the tiniest sprout;*
The terrace of nine stories rises from a mound of earth;
The journey of a thousand miles commences with a
*   single step.*
He who acts does harm.
He who takes hold of a thing loses his hold.
The sage does not act, and therefore does no harm;
He does not take hold, and therefore does not lose
*   his hold.*
People repeatedly fail when they are on the eve of success.
If they were careful at the end, as at the beginning,
They would not so ruin them.
Therefore the sage turns his back on desire.

He does not prize things difficult to get;
He learns to forget what he has learned;
And he turns back to what the multitude have already lost.
Thus he helps the natural development of all things,
By not taking action.

LI SSU

MEMORIAL ON ANNEXATION OF FEUDAL STATES

Taking advantage of critical opportunities. Advice to a leader.

He who waits for others misses his opportunities.

A man aiming at great achievements takes advantage of a critical juncture and relentlessly follows it through.

Why is it that during all the years that Duke Mu of Ch'in was chief among the feudal princes, he did not try to annex the Six States to the east? It was because the feudal lords were still numerous and the power of the imperial Chou had not yet decayed.

Hence, as the Five Overlords succeeded one another, each in turn upheld the House of Chou. But since the time of Duke Hsiao of Ch'in the House of Chou has been declining, the feudal states have been annexing one another, and east of the pass there remain only Six States.

Through military victories, the State of Ch'in has, in the time of the last six kings, brought the feudal lords into submission. And by now the feudal states yield obeisance to Ch'in.

Now, with the might of Ch'in and the virtues of Your Highness, at one stroke, like sweeping off the dust from a kitchen stove, the feudal lords can be annihilated, imperial rule can be established, and unification of the world can be brought about.

This is the one moment in ten thousand ages.

If Your Highness allows it to slip away and does not press the advantage in haste, the feudal lords will revive their strength and organize themselves into an anti-Ch'in alliance. Then no one, even though he possessed the virtues of the Yellow Emperor, would be able to annex their territories.

CHU HSI

ON THE DOCTRINE OF THE MEAN

Omens and divination. Trust in foreknowledge.

It is characteristic of absolute sincerity to be able to anticipate the future.

When a nation or family is about to flourish, there are sure to be lucky omens.

When a nation or family is about to perish, there are sure to be unlucky omens.

These omens are revealed in divination and in the movements of the four limbs. When calamity or blessing is about to come, one can surely know beforehand if it is good, and one can also surely know beforehand if it is evil.

Therefore he who has absolute faith is like a spirit.

Chapter Five

STRATEGY AND CONFLICT

SUN TZU

THE ART OF WAR

Elements of calculation and deception.

The art of war is of vital importance to the state. It is a matter of life and death, a road either to safety or to ruin. Hence it is a subject for study that can on no account be neglected.

The art of war is governed by five constant factors, all of which need to be considered. These are: The Way, Heaven, Earth, the Commander, and Discipline.

- The Way causes the people to be in complete accord with their ruler, so that they will follow him regardless of their lives, undismayed by any danger.

- Heaven signifies night and day, cold and heat, seasons, and cycles of the moon.
- Earth comprises distances, great and small; danger and security; open ground and narrow passes; the chances of life and death.
- The Commander stands for the virtues of wisdom, sincerity, benevolence, courage, and strictness.
- Discipline is to be understood as the marshaling of the army in its proper subdivisions, the gradations of rank among the officers, the maintenance of roads by which supplies may reach the army, and the control of military expenditure.

These five factors should be familiar to every general. He who knows them will be victorious. He who knows them not will fail.

Therefore, when seeking to determine the military conditions, make your decisions on the basis of comparison, utilizing the seven considerations, in this wise:

1. Which of the two sovereigns is imbued with the Way?
2. Which of the two generals has the most ability?
3. With whom lie the advantages derived from Heaven and Earth?
4. On which side is Discipline most rigorously enforced?
5. Which army is the stronger?
6. On which side are officers and men more highly trained?

7. In which army is there the greater constancy, both in reward and in punishment?

By means of these seven considerations I can forecast victory or defeat.

The general who hearkens to my counsel and acts upon it will conquer—let such a one be retained in command! The general who hearkens not to my counsel, nor acts upon it will suffer defeat—let such a one be dismissed!

While heeding the profit of my counsel, avail yourself also of any helpful circumstances over and beyond the ordinary rules. Plans should be modified to reflect favorable or unfavorable circumstances.

All warfare is based on deception. Hence, when able to attack, we must seem unable. When using our forces, we must seem inactive. When we are near, we must make the enemy believe we are far away. When far away, we must make him believe we are near. Hold out baits to entice the enemy. Feign disorder, and crush him. If he is secure at all points, be prepared for him. If he is superior in strength, evade him. If your opponent is quick to anger, seek to irritate him. Pretend to be weak, that he may grow arrogant. If he is taking his ease, give him no rest. If his forces are united, separate them. Attack him where he is unprepared. Appear where you are not expected.

These military devices lead to victory, and they must not be divulged beforehand.

The general who wins a battle makes many calculations in his temple before the battle is fought. The general who loses the battle makes only a few calculations beforehand. Thus do many calculations lead to victory, and few calculations to defeat. How much more no calculation at all! It is by attention to this point that I can foresee who is likely to win or lose.

The economics of war, and the importance of speed.

In the operations of war, where there are in the field a thousand swift chariots, a thousand heavy chariots, and a hundred thousand mail-clad soldiers, with provisions enough to carry them a thousand miles, the expenditure at home and at the front, including entertainment of guests, small items such as glue and paint, and sums spent on chariots and armor, will reach the total of a thousand ounces of silver per day. Such is the cost of raising an army of a hundred thousand men.

When you engage in actual fighting, if victory is long in coming, the men's weapons will grow dull and their ardor will be dampened. If you lay siege to a town, you will exhaust your strength. If the campaign is protracted, the resources of the state will not be equal to the strain. When your weapons are dulled, your ardor dampened, your strength exhausted, and your treasure spent, other chieftains will spring up to take advantage of your extremity. Then no man, however wise, will be able to avert the inevitable consequences.

Thus, though we have heard of stupid haste in war, cleverness has never been seen associated with long delays.

There is no instance of a country having benefited from prolonged warfare. Only one who knows the disastrous effects of a long war can realize the supreme importance of speed in bringing it to a close.

The skillful leader does not raise a second levy; neither are his supply wagons loaded more than twice. Once war is declared, he will not waste precious time in waiting for reinforcements, nor will he turn his army back for fresh supplies. He will cross the enemy's frontier with no delay.

Now, in order to kill the enemy, our men must be roused to anger. That there may be advantage from defeating the enemy, they must have their rewards.

Therefore in chariot fighting, when ten or more chariots have been taken, those should be rewarded who took the first. Our own flags should be substituted for those of the enemy, and the chariots mingled and used in conjunction with ours. The captured soldiers should be kindly treated and kept. This is called using the conquered foe to augment one's own strength.

In war, then, let your objective be victory, not lengthy campaigns. Thus it may be known that the leader of armies is the arbiter of the people's fate, the man on whom it depends whether the nation shall be in peace or in peril.

Basic strategies, not fighting at all, and essentials for victory.

In the practical art of war, the best thing of all is to take the enemy's country whole and intact. To shatter and destroy is not so good. So, too, it is better to capture an army than to destroy it. It is better to capture a whole regiment, an entire detachment, or a full company, than to destroy them.

So, to fight and conquer in all your battles is not supreme excellence. Supreme excellence consists in breaking the enemy's resistance without fighting.

Thus the highest form of leadership is to thwart the enemy's plans. The next best is to prevent the junction of the enemy's forces. The next in order is to attack the enemy's army in the field. And the worst policy of all is to besiege walled cities. The rule is not to besiege walled cities if it can possibly be avoided, for the preparation of defensive screens, movable shelters, and various implements of war will take up three whole months; and the piling up of mounds over against the walls will take three months more. The general, unable to control his irritation, will launch his men to the assault like swarming ants, with the result that one third of his men are slain, while the town still remains untaken. Such are the disastrous effects of a siege.

Therefore the skillful leader subdues the enemy's troops without any fighting. He captures their cities without laying siege to them. He overthrows their kingdom without lengthy operations in the field. With his forces intact he disputes the mastery of the empire, and without losing a man, his triumph is complete. And the weapon, not being blunted by use, remains sharp and perfect.

This is the method of attacking by stratagem.

This is the rule in war:

- If our forces are ten to the enemy's one, surround him.
- If our forces are five to his one, attack him.
- If equally matched, we can offer battle.
- If slightly inferior in numbers, we can avoid the enemy.
- If quite unequal to the enemy in every way, we can flee from him.

Though an obstinate fight may be made by a small force, in the end it must be captured by the larger force.

The general is the bulwark of the state. If the bulwark is strong at all points, the state will be strong. If the bulwark is defective, the state will be weak.

There are three ways in which a sovereign can bring misfortune upon his general and his army:

1. By commanding the army to advance or to retreat, being ignorant of the fact that it cannot obey. This is called hobbling the army.
2. By attempting to govern an army in the same way as he administers a kingdom, being ignorant of the conditions that obtain in an army. This causes restlessness in the soldiers' minds.
3. By employing the officers of his army without discrimination, through ignorance of the military principle of adaptation to circumstances. This shakes the confidence of the soldiers, and when the army is

restless and distrustful, trouble is sure to come from the other feudal princes. This is simply bringing anarchy into the army, and flinging victory away.

Thus we may know that there are five essentials for victory.

1. He will win who knows when to fight and when not to fight.
2. He will win who knows how to handle both superior and inferior forces.
3. He will win whose army is animated by the same spirit throughout all its ranks.
4. He will win who, prepared himself, waits to take the enemy unprepared.
5. He will win who has military capacity and is not interfered with by the sovereign.

Victory lies in the knowledge of these five points. Hence the saying: If you know the enemy and know yourself, you need not fear the result of a hundred battles. If you know yourself but not the enemy, for every victory gained you will suffer a defeat. If you know neither the enemy nor yourself, you will succumb in every battle.

Divine manipulation of the threads: the use of spies.

Raising a host of a hundred thousand men and marching them great distances entails heavy loss on the people and a drain on the resources of the state. The daily expenditure will amount to a thousand ounces of silver. There will be commotion at home and abroad, and men will drop down exhausted on the highways. As many as seven hundred thousand families will be impeded in their labor.

Hostile armies may face each other for years, striving for the victory that is decided in a single day. This being so, to remain in ignorance of the enemy's condition, simply because one grudges the outlay of a hundred ounces of silver in honors and fees, is the height of inhumanity.

One who acts thus is no leader of men, no help to his sovereign, and no master of victory.

What enables the wise sovereign and the good general to strike and conquer, achieving things beyond the reach of ordinary men, is foreknowledge. Now this foreknowledge cannot be elicited from spirits. It cannot be obtained inductively from experience, nor by any deductive calculation.

Knowledge of the enemy's dispositions can only be obtained from other men.

Hence the use of spies, of whom there are five classes: local spies, internal spies, converted spies, doomed spies, surviving spies.

When these five kinds of spies are all at work, none can discover the secret system.

This is called "divine manipulation of the threads."

It is the sovereign's most precious faculty.

Having local spies means employing the services of the inhabitants of a district.

Having inward spies means making use of officials of the enemy.

Having converted spies means getting hold of the enemy's spies and using them for our own purposes.

Having doomed spies means doing certain things openly for purposes of deception, and allowing our own spies to know of them and report them to the enemy.

Surviving spies, finally, are those who bring back news from the enemy's camp.

Hence it follows there must be no more intimate relations in the whole army than those maintained with spies. No one should be more liberally rewarded. And nowhere else should greater secrecy be preserved.

Spies cannot be usefully employed without a certain intuitive sagacity.

Spies cannot be properly managed without benevolence and directness.

Without subtle ingenuity of mind, one cannot make certain of the truth of their reports.

Be subtle! Be subtle! And use your spies for every kind of business.

If a secret piece of news is divulged by a spy before the time is ripe, he must be put to death together with the person to whom the secret was told.

Whether the object be to crush an army, to storm a city, or to assassinate an individual, it is always necessary to begin by finding out the names of the attendants, the aides-de-camp, the doorkeepers and sentries of the general in command. Our spies must be commissioned to ascertain these.

The enemy's spies who have come to spy on us must be sought out, tempered with bribes, led away, and comfortably housed. Thus they will become converted spies and available for our service.

It is through the information brought by the converted spy that we are able to acquire and employ local and inward spies. It is owing to his information, again, that we can cause the doomed spy to carry false tidings to the enemy. Lastly, it is by his information that the surviving spy can be used on appointed occasions.

The end and aim of spying in all its five varieties is knowledge of the enemy. And this knowledge can only be derived, in the first instance, from the converted spy. Hence it is essential that the converted spy be treated with the utmost liberality.

Of old, the rise of the Yin dynasty was due to I Chi, who had served under the Hsia. Likewise, the rise of the Chou dynasty was due to Lu Ya, who had served under the Yin.

Hence it is only the enlightened ruler and the wise general who will use the highest intelligence of the army for purposes of spying, and thereby they achieve great results.

Spies are a most important element in war, because upon them depends an army's ability to move.

CHANG YU

On planning.

While the main laws of strategy can be stated clearly enough for the benefit of all, you must be guided by the actions of the enemy in attempting to secure a favorable position in actual warfare.

MEI YAO-CH'EN

COMMENTARY ON *THE ART OF WAR*

On foreknowledge and spies.

Knowledge of the spirit world is to be obtained by divination. Information in natural science may be sought by inductive reasoning. The laws of the universe can be verified by mathematical calculation. But the dispositions of the enemy are ascertainable through spies and spies alone.

CHIA LIN

On the use of spies.

An army without spies is like a man without ears or eyes.

LAO TZU

TAO TE CHING

Seriousness and responsiveness in conflict.

There is a military saying:
I do not dare to make the first move;
I prefer to be the guest.
I do not dare to advance an inch;
I prefer to retire a foot.
This is called marshaling the ranks where there are no
*   ranks to be seen;*
Baring the arms where there are no arms shown;
Grasping the weapon where there is no visible weapon
*   to grasp;*
Advancing against the enemy without seeming to move.
There is no calamity greater than lightly engaging in war.
To do that is near losing all that is precious.
Thus it is that when opposing weapons are crossed,
He who is most serious conquers.

CHUANG TZU

Emptiness as a form of self-defense.

If a man is crossing a river in a boat, and an empty vessel comes into collision with it, even though he be a man of a choleric temper, he will not be angry with it.

If there be a person, however, in that boat, he will yell out to him to haul out of the way. If his shout is not heard, he will repeat it; and if the other does not then hear, he will call out a third time, following up the shout with abusive terms.

Formerly he was not angry, but now he is. Formerly he thought the boat was empty, but now there is a person in it. If a man can empty himself of himself during his time in the world, who can harm him?

Protection that is self-defeating.

In taking precautions against thieves who cut open satchels and search bags, and break open boxes, people are sure to cord and fasten them well, and to employ strong bonds and clasps; and in this they are ordinarily said to show their wisdom.

When a great thief comes, however, he shoulders the box, lifts up the satchel, carries off the bag, and runs away with them, afraid only that the cords, bonds, and clasps may not be secure. In this case what was called the wisdom of the owners proves to be nothing but a collecting of the things for the great thief.

Let me try and set this matter forth. Do not those who are vulgarly called wise prove to be collectors for the great thieves? And do not those who are called sages prove to be but guardians in the interest of the great thieves?

How do I know that the case is so? Formerly, in the state of Khi, the neighboring towns could see one another.

Their cocks and dogs never ceased to answer the crowing and barking of other cocks and dogs. The nets were set in the water and on the land; and the plows and hoes were employed over more than a space of two thousand square miles. All within its four boundaries, the establishment of the ancestral temples and of the altars of the land and grain, and the ordering of the hamlets and houses, and of every corner in the districts, large, medium, and small, were in all particulars according to the rules of the sages.

So it was.

But yet one morning, Thien Khang-tze killed the ruler of Khi, and stole his state.

And was it only the state that he stole? Along with it he stole also the regulations of the sages and wise men observed in it.

And so, though he got the name of being a thief and a robber, he himself continued to live securely. Small states did not dare to find fault with him. Great states did not dare to take him off. For twelve generations his descendants have possessed the state of Khi.

Thus do we not have a case in which not only did the party steal the state of Khi, but at the same time the regulations of its sages and wise men, which thereby served to guard the person of him, thief and robber as he was?

Chapter Six

NEGOTIATING AND SELLING

CONFUCIUS

ANALECTS

"First kill all the lawyers."

"In *hearing* causes, I am like other men," said the Master. "The great point is—to *prevent* litigation."

Timing the deal.

Tzu-Kung once said to the Master, "Here's a fine gem. Would you guard it carefully in a casket and store it away, or seek a good price for it and sell it?"

"Sell it, indeed," said the Master. "But I should wait for the bidder."

LAO TZU

TAO TE CHING

Silence is golden.

> He who knows does not speak.
> He who speaks does not know.
> Keep the mouth shut,
> And close the senses.
> Blunt sharp points,
> And simplify all things.
> Make brightness,
> And become one with the lowest.
> This is called primal union.
> One who has achieved this
> Cares nothing for friends or enemies.
> He is beyond all consideration of profit or injury,
> Honor or disgrace.
> He is the noblest man under Heaven.

The virtue of passivity. The trouble with striving.

> The fact that the sea
> Is able to receive the tribute of all the valley streams
> Is its virtue in being below them.
> The sea is thus the king of them all.
> So it is that the sage, wishing to be above men,
> Puts himself by his words below them,
> And, wishing to be before them,
> Places his person behind them.

In this way, though he has his place above them,
Men do not feel his weight;
Nor though he has his place before them,
Do they feel it an injury to them.
Therefore all in the world delight to exalt him
And do not weary of him.
Because he does not strive,
No one finds it possible to strive with him.

Against argument. In favor of giving.

Truthful words are not fine.
Fine words are not truthful.
Virtuous men do not argue;
Those who argue are not good.
Those who know are not learned;
The learned do not know.
The sage does not accumulate.
The more he does for others, the more he possesses.
The more he gives to others, the more he has for himself.
The Way of Heaven is sharp, but it injures not;
The Way of the sage is to do without doing.

Aftermath of negotiation. Agreements and contracts.

When a reconciliation is effected after a great animosity,
There is sure to be a grudge remaining.
What is to be done?
To guard against this, the sage keeps his half of the   .
*   agreement,*

And does not insist on fulfillment of it by the other party.
So, a virtuous man honors the agreement,
While the man without virtue exacts fulfillment from
      others.
In the Way of Heaven, there is no partiality of love;
It is always on the side of the good man.

CHUANG TZU

Recognizing value and capitalizing on it.

Hui-tzu spoke to Chuang-tzu, saying,

"The king of Wei sent me some seeds of a large calabash, which I sowed. The fruit, when fully grown, could contain five gallons of anything I wanted. I used it to contain water, but it was so heavy that I could not lift it by myself. I cut it in two to make the parts into drinking vessels; but the dried shells were too wide and unstable and would not hold the liquid; nothing but large useless things! Because of their uselessness I knocked them to pieces."

Chuang-tzu replied,

"You were indeed stupid, my master, in the use of what was large.

"There was a man of Sung who was skillful at making a salve which kept the hands from getting chapped; and his family for generations had made the bleaching of cocoon-silk their business.

"A stranger heard of it, and proposed to buy the art of the preparation for a hundred ounces of silver. The kindred all came together, and considered the proposal. 'We have,' said they, 'been bleaching cocoon-silk for generations, and have only gained a little money. Now in one morning we can sell to this man our art for a hundred ounces; let him have it.'

"The stranger accordingly got it and went away with it to give counsel to the king of Wu, who was then engaged in hostilities with Yueh. As a reward, the king gave him the command of his fleet, and in the winter he had an engagement with that of Yueh, on which he inflicted a great defeat, and was invested with a portion of territory taken from Yueh.

"Keeping the hands from getting chapped was the same in both cases; but in the one case it led to the investiture of the possessor of the salve, and in the other it had only enabled its owners to continue their bleaching. The difference of result was owing to the different use made of the art.

"Now you, Sir, had calabashes large enough to hold five gallons. Why did you not think of making large bottle-gourds of them, by means of which you could have floated over rivers and lakes, instead of giving yourself the sorrow of finding that they were useless for holding anything?

"Your mind, my master, would seem to have been closed against all intelligence!"

Hui-tzu said to Chuang-tzu,

"I have a large tree, which men call the Ailanthus. Its trunk swells out to a large size but is not fit for a carpenter to apply his line to it; its smaller branches are knotted and crooked, so that the disk and square cannot be used on them. Though planted on the wayside, a builder would not turn his head to look at it. Now your words, Sir, are great but of no use."

Chuang-tzu replied,

"Have you never seen a wild cat or a weasel? There it lies, crouching and low, till the wanderer approaches; east and west it leaps about, avoiding neither what is high nor what is low, till it is caught in a trap, or dies in a net.

"Again there is the yak, so large that it is like a cloud hanging in the sky. It is large indeed, but it cannot catch mice.

"You, Sir, have a large tree and are troubled because it is of no use. Why do you not plant it in a tract where there is nothing else, or in a wide and barren wild? There you might saunter idly by its side, or in the enjoyment of untroubled ease sleep beneath it. Neither saw nor ax would shorten its existence; there would be nothing to injure it.

"What is there in its uselessness to cause you distress?"

The customer is always right. The tax-collector's story.

Pei-kung She was collecting taxes for Duke Ling of Wei, to be employed in the making of bells.

In connection with the work he built an altar outside the gate of the suburban wall.

In three months the bells were completed, even to the suspending of the upper and lower tiers.

The king's son, Khing-ki, saw them, and asked what arts he had employed in the making of them.

He replied, "Besides my undivided attention to them, I did not venture to use any arts. I have heard the saying, 'After all the carving and the chiseling, let the object be to return to simplicity.' I was as a child who has no knowledge. I was extraordinarily slow and hesitating. They grew like the springing plants, of themselves.

"In escorting those who went, and meeting those who came, my object was neither to hinder the comers nor detain the goers. I suffered those who strongly opposed to take their way, and accepted those who did their best to come to terms. I allowed them all to do the utmost they could, and in this way morning and evening I collected the taxes. I did not have the slightest trouble, and how much more will this be the case with those who pursue the Great Way on a grand scale!"

Chapter Seven

EMPLOYEES
AND BOSSES
(HUMAN RESOURCES)

CONFUCIUS

ANALECTS

Meditations on colleagues at all levels.

When the year grows chilly we know the pine and cypress are the last to fade. (Good men are like evergreens.)

———

The noble-minded man makes the most of others' good qualities, not the worst of their bad ones. Men of small mind do the reverse of this.

———

When we see men of worth, we should think of equaling them. When we see men of a contrary character, we should turn inward and examine ourselves.

———

Where the solid qualities are in excess of accomplishments, we have rusticity; where the accomplishments are in excess of the solid qualities, we have the manners of a clerk. When the accomplishments and solid qualities are equally blended, we then have the man of virtue.

———

The superior man may not be conversant with petty details, and yet may have important matters put into his hands. The inferior man may not be charged with important matters, yet may be conversant with the petty details.

———

In serving your prince, make your service your serious concern, and let payment be a secondary matter.

Practical advice for the worker.

The Master said,

"He who is not in any particular office has nothing to do with plans for the administration of its duties."

———

There are three errors into which they who wait upon their superior may fall:

1. to speak before the opportunity comes to them to speak, which I call heedless haste.
2. refraining from speaking when the opportunity has come, which I call concealment.
3. speaking, regardless of the mood he is in, which I call blindness.

———

Tze-lu asked whether he should immediately carry into practice what he heard.

The Master said, "There are your father and elder brothers to be consulted; why should you act on that principle of immediately carrying into practice what you hear?"

Zan Yu asked the same, whether he should immediately carry into practice what he heard.

And the Master answered, "Immediately carry into practice what you hear."

Kung-hsi Hwa said, "Yu asked whether he should carry immediately into practice what he heard, and you said, 'There are your father and elder brothers to be consulted.' Ch'iu asked whether he should immediately carry into practice what he heard, and you said, 'Carry it immediately into practice.' I, Chi'ih, am perplexed, and venture to ask you for an explanation."

The Master said, "Ch'iu is retiring and slow; therefore I urged him forward. Yu has more than his own share of energy; therefore, I kept him back."

The varieties of ambition.

Tze-lu, Tsang Hsi, Zan Yu, and Kung-hsi Hwa were sitting by the Master.

He said to them, "Though I am a day or so older than you, do not think of that.

"From day to day you are saying, 'We are not known.'

"If some ruler were to know you, what would you like to do?"

Tze-lu hastily and lightly replied, "Suppose the case of a state of ten thousand chariots. Let it be in peril from other large states around it. Let it be suffering from invading armies. And to this let there be added a famine in corn and in all vegetables.

"If I were entrusted with the government of it, in three years time I could make the people to be bold, and to recognize the rule of righteous conduct."

The Master smiled at him.

Turning to Zan Yu, the Master said, "Ch'iu, what are your wishes?"

Ch'iu replied, "Suppose a state of sixty or seventy square miles, and let me have the government of it. In three years time, I could make plenty to abound among the people. As to teaching them the principles of propriety, and music, I must wait for the rise of a superior man to do that."

"What are your wishes, Chi'ih?" said the Master next to Kung-hsi Hwa.

Chi'ih replied, "I do not say that my ability extends to these things, but I should wish to learn them. At the services of the ancestral temple, and at the audiences of the princes with the sovereign, I should like, dressed in the dark square-made robe and the black linen cap, to act as a small assistant."

Last of all, the Master asked Tsang Hsi, "Tien, what are your wishes?"

Tien, pausing as he was playing on his lute, while it was yet twanging, laid the instrument aside and rose.

"My wishes," he said, "are different from the cherished purposes of these three gentlemen."

"What harm is there in that?" said the Master. "Please, as they already have, speak out your wishes."

Tien then said, "In this, the last month of spring, with the dress of the season all complete, along with five or six of my friends, I would wish to wash in the river, enjoy the breeze among the rain altars, and return to my singing."

The Master heaved a sigh and said, "I give my approval to Tien."

Advice for middle management.

The superior man, having obtained their confidence, may then impose labors on his people. If he has not gained their confidence, they will think that he is oppressing them. Having obtained the confidence of his prince, one may then remonstrate with him. If he has not gained his confidence, the prince will think that he is vilifying him.

LAO TZU

Tao Te Ching

Non-interference.

When the people do not fear what they ought to fear,
That which is their great dread will come on them.
Do not intrude in their life or their work;

It is by avoiding such intrusion that weariness does
not arise.
Therefore the sage knows himself,
But does not parade his knowledge;
He has self-respect, but does not set a value on himself.
And thus he puts one thing away and chooses another.

CHUANG TZU

Proper division of labor.

Originating belongs to those in the higher position; the details of work, to those who are in the lower.

The compendious decision belongs to the lord; the minutiae of execution, to his ministers.

The direction of the three hosts and their men with the five weapons is but a trifling quality.

Rewards and penalties with their advantages and sufferings, and the inflictions of the five punishments are but trivial elements of instruction.

Ceremonies, laws, measures, and numbers, with all the minutiae of jurisprudence, are small matters in government.

The notes of bells and drums, and the display of plumes and flags are the slightest things in music.

And the various grades of the mourning garments are the most unimportant manifestations of grief.

These five unimportant adjuncts required the operation

of the excited spirit and the employment of the arts of the mind, to bring them into use. The men of old had them indeed, but they did not give them the first place.

The ruler precedes, and the minister follows. The father precedes, and the son follows. The elder brother precedes, and the younger follows. The senior precedes, and the junior follows. The male precedes, and the female follows. The husband precedes, and the wife follows.

The precedence of the more honorable and sequence of the meaner is seen in the action of Heaven and Earth, and hence the sages took them as their pattern.

The more honorable position of Heaven and the lower one of Earth are equivalent to a designation of their spirit-like and intelligent qualities.

The precedence of spring and summer and the sequence of autumn and winter mark the order of the four seasons.

In the transformations and growth of all things, every bud and branch has its proper form. And in this we have their gradual maturing and decay, the constant flow of transformation and change.

Thus, since Heaven and Earth, which are most spirit-like, are distinguished as more honorable and less, and by precedence and sequence, how much more must we look for this in the ways of men!

In the ancestral temple it is to kinship that honor is given. In the neighborhoods and districts, honor is given to age. In the conduct of business, honor is given to wisdom.

Such is the order in those great ways. If we speak of the course, and do not observe it, why do we apply that name to it?

Situations that preclude success.

Yen Hui went to see the Master, and asked leave to take his departure.

"Where are you going?" asked the Master.

"I will go to Wei," was the reply.

"And with what object?"

"I have heard that the ruler of Wei is in the vigor of his years, and consults none but himself as to his course. He deals with his state as if it were a light matter, and has no perception of his errors. He thinks lightly of his people's dying. The dead are lying all over the country as if no smaller space could contain them; on the plains and about the marshes, they are as thick as heaps of fuel. The people know not where to turn. I have heard you, Master, say, 'Leave the state that is well governed; go to the state where disorder prevails.' At the door of a physician there are many who are ill. I wish through what I have heard from you to think out some methods of dealing with Wei, if peradventure the evils of the state may be cured."

The Master said, "Alas! The risk is that you will go only to suffer in the punishment of yourself. The perfect men of old first had what they wanted to do in themselves, and afterward they found the response to it in others. If what they wanted in themselves was not fixed, what leisure had they to go and interfere with the proceedings of any tyrannous man?

"Moreover, do you know how virtue is liable to be dissipated, and how wisdom proceeds to display itself? Virtue is dissipated in the pursuit of the name for it, and wisdom seeks to display itself in striving with others. In the pursuit of the name, men overthrow one another; wisdom becomes a weapon of contention. Both these things are instruments of evil, and should not be allowed to have free course in one's conduct.

"Supposing one's virtue to be great and his faith firm, what if he does not comprehend the spirit of those whom he wishes to influence?

"And supposing he is free from the disposition to strive for reputation, what if he does not comprehend their minds?

"When in such a case he forcibly insists on benevolence and righteousness, setting them forth in the strongest and most direct language before the tyrant, then that tyrant, hating his reprover's possession of those excellent qualities, will put him down as doing him injury.

"He who injures others is sure to be injured by them in return. You indeed will hardly escape being injured by the man to whom you go!

"Further, if perchance he takes pleasure in men of worth and hates those of an opposite character, what is the use of your seeking to make yourself out to be different from such men about him? Before you have begun to announce your views, he, as king and ruler, will take advantage of you, and immediately contend with you for victory.

"Your eyes will be dazed and full of perplexity. You will try to look pleased with him. You will frame your words with care. Your demeanor will be conformed to his. You will confirm him in his views.

"In this way you will be adding fire to fire, and water to water, increasing, as we may express it, the evils which you deplore. To these signs of deferring to him at the first there will be no end. You will be in danger, seeing he does not believe you, of making your words more strong, and you are sure to die at the hands of such a tyrant.

"Formerly Kieh killed Kwan Lung-fang, and Kau killed the prince Pi-kan. Both of these cultivated their persons, bending down in sympathy with the lower people to comfort them in their suffering from oppressors, and on their account opposing their superiors. On this account, because they so ordered their conduct, their rulers contrived their destruction, such regard had they for their own fame.

"Yao anciently attacked the states of Dhung-kih and Hsu-ao, and Yu attacked the ruler of Hu. Those states were left empty, with no one to continue their population, the people being exterminated. They had engaged in war without ceasing. Their craving for whatever they could get was insatiable.

"And this ruler of Wei is, like them, one who craves after fame and greater substance. Have you not heard it? Those sages were not able to overcome his thirst for fame and substance. How much less will you be able to do so!

"Nevertheless you must have some ground for the course which you wish to take. Pray try and tell it to me."

Yen Hui said, "May I go, doing so in uprightness and humility, using also every endeavor to be uniform in my plans of operation?"

"No, indeed!" was the reply. "How can you do so? This man makes a display of being filled to overflowing with virtue, and has great self-conceit. His feelings are not to be determined from his countenance. Ordinary men do not venture to oppose him, and he proceeds from the way in which he affects them to seek still more the satisfaction of his own mind. He may be described as unaffected by the small lessons of virtue brought to bear on him from day to day. And how much less will he be so by your great lessons? He will be obstinate, and refuse to be converted. He may outwardly agree with you, but inwardly there will be no self-condemnation. How can you go to him in this way and be successful?"

Yen Hui rejoined, "Well, then; while inwardly maintaining my straightforward intention, I will outwardly seem to bend to him. I will deliver my lessons, and substantiate them by appealing to antiquity. Inwardly maintaining my straightforward intention, I shall be a co-worker with Heaven.

"Outwardly bending, I shall be a co-worker with other men. To carry the memorandum tablet to court, to kneel, and to bend the body reverentially: These are the observances of ministers. They all employ them, and should I presume not to do so? Doing what other men do, they would have no occasion to blame me. This is what is called being a fellow-worker with other men.

"Fully declaring my sentiments and substantiating them by appealing to antiquity, I shall be a co-worker with the ancients. Although the words in which I convey my lessons may really be condemnatory of the ruler, they will be those of antiquity, and not my own. In this way, though straightforward, I shall be free from blame. This is what is called being a co-worker with antiquity.

"May I go to Wei in this way, and be successful?"

"No, indeed!" said the Master. "How can you do so? You have too many plans of proceeding, and have not spied out the ruler's character. Though you firmly adhere to your plans, you may be held free from transgression, but this will be all the result. How can you in this way produce the transformation which you desire? All this only shows in you the mind of a teacher!"

Self-promotion and modesty.

Yang-tzu, having gone to Sung, passed the night in a lodging-house, the master of which had two concubines, one beautiful, the other ugly. The ugly one was honored, however, and the beautiful one despised.

Yang-tzu asked the reason, and a little boy of the house replied, "The beauty knows her beauty, and we do not recognize it. The ugly one knows her ugliness, and we do not recognize it."

Yang-tzu said, "Remember this, my disciples. Act virtuously, and put away the practice of priding yourselves on your virtue. If you do this, where can you go to that you will not be loved?"

TU MU

COMMENTARY ON *THE ART OF WAR*

The value of rewards.

Rewards are necessary in order to make the soldiers see the advantage of beating the enemy. Thus, when you capture spoils from the enemy, they must be used as rewards, so that all your men may have a keen desire to fight, each on his own account.

Non-discrimination in employment.

The skillful employer of men will employ the wise man, the brave man, the covetous man, and the stupid man. For the wise man delights in establishing his merit, the brave man likes to show his courage in action, the covetous man is quick at seizing advantages, and the stupid man has no fear of death.

HAN FEI TZU

Six Contrarieties

Evaluations. A further argument for non-discrimination.

If all men are asleep, a blind man among them will not be noticed.

If all men are silent, no mute among them will be detected.

Awake them and ask each what he sees, or question them and ask each one to reply.

Then both the blind and the mute will be discovered.

Likewise, unless their speeches are heard, the foolish will not be known.

Unless appointed to office, the unworthy will not be exposed.

Heed their speeches and seek their truth. Appoint them to office and hold them responsible for the results of their work.

Then both the foolish and the unworthy will be discovered.

Indeed, when you need wrestlers, if you merely listen to their own words, then you cannot distinguish between a loser and champion.

Given tripods and bowls, then both the weak and the strong come to the fore.

Similarly, official posts are the tripods and bowls to able men.

Entrusted with affairs, the stupid and the intelligent will be differentiated.

As a result, the foolish will not be used and the unworthy will not be appointed to office.

Chapter Eight

RANK
AND
PROMOTION

CONFUCIUS

ANALECTS

Trust quality to shine.

Chung-kung, on being made first minister to the Chief of the Ki family, consulted the Master about government.

To him the Master said, "Let the heads of offices *be* heads. Excuse small faults. Promote men of sagacity and talent."

"But," he asked, "how am I to know the sagacious and talented, before promoting them?"

"Promote those whom you do know," said the Master. "As to those of whom you are uncertain, will *others* not notice them?"

MO TZU

THE EXALTATION OF MEN OF WORTH

Honor, praise, and rewards.

Today kings, dukes, and the leaders of society, in making systems of government, all want the country to be rich, the population big, and the administration of justice such as to produce order.

But instead of getting wealth they get poverty, instead of a big population a small one, instead of order disorder. This then is basically to miss what they want and get what they hate. What are the facts about this matter?

Disorder consists in the failure of the kings, dukes, and other leaders to promote men of worth and use the services of able men in administration.

The facts are that if a country has plenty of worthy officers, then the order provided by the state is an unbreakable one. If it has few such officers, then its order is easily broken. Thus it is that the business of leadership consists primarily in increasing the number of men of worth.

To illustrate, if you want to increase the number of expert archers and drivers in the country, you will certainly have to enrich them, elevate their social status, honor them, and praise them before you can obtain a full complement of them.

How much more does this apply to worthy officers, to men of solid virtue, with a command of language, learned in the method of the Way?

These, to be sure, are the treasures of the state, the assistants of its guardian deities. These also must be enriched, have their social status enhanced. They should be honored and praised before a country's full complement of worthy officers can be reached.

When the Sage-kings of antiquity began to govern, their word was:

"The unrighteous shall not be enriched, the unrighteous shall not be ennobled, the unrighteous shall not have court favor, the unrighteous shall not stand near the royal person."

The rich and noble, when they heard this, all retired and consulted to this effect:

"We originally depended on our wealth and station, and now our lord promotes the righteous regardless of whether they are poor and baseborn. That being so, it follows that we must on no account be unrighteous."

In those days, therefore, there was a hierarchy of virtue and rewards on the basis of work done. Officials were not permanently ennobled and the rank and file endlessly at the bottom of the social scale. The man of ability was elevated, the man of no ability put below him. Public spirit was encouraged, and personal grudges put away.

CHUANG TZU

The person is not the job. The job is not the person.

Kien Wu spoke to Sun-shu Aio, saying, "You, Sir, were thrice chief minister, and did not feel elated. You were thrice dismissed from that position, without manifesting any sorrow. At first I was in doubt about you, but I am not now, since I see how regularly and quietly the breath comes through your nostrils. How is it that you exercise your mind?"

Sun-shu Aio replied, "In what do I surpass other men? When the position came to me, I thought it should not be rejected. When it was taken away, I thought it could not be retained. I considered that the getting or losing of it did not make me what I was, and was no occasion for any manifestation of sorrow. That was all. In what did I surpass other men?

"Moreover, I did not know whether the honor of it belonged to the dignity of the position, or to myself. If it belonged to the position, it was nothing to me; if it belonged to me, it had nothing to do with the position.

"While occupied with these uncertainties, and looking round in all directions, what leisure had I to take knowledge of whether men honored me or thought me mean?"

The dangers of outstanding merit and distinction.

The king of Wu, floating about on the River Kiang, landed and ascended the hill of monkeys, all of which, when they saw him, scampered off in terror, and hid themselves among the thick hazels.

There was one, however, which, in an unconcerned way, swung about on the branches, displaying its cleverness to the king, who thereon discharged an arrow at it. With a nimble motion it caught the swift arrow in its fist.

Seeing this exhibition of skill, the king ordered his attendants to hurry forward and destroy it.

Thus the monkey was seized and killed.

The king then, looking round, said to his friend Yen Pu-i, "This monkey made a display of its artfulness, and trusted in its agility, to show me its arrogance. This it was which brought it to this fate. Take warning from it. Do not by your looks give yourself haughty airs!"

Yen Pu-i, when he returned home, put himself under the teaching of Tung Wu, to root up his pride. He put away what he delighted in and abjured distinction.

In three years the people of the kingdom spoke of him with admiration.

Chapter Nine

EDUCATION
AND
IMPROVEMENT

CONFUCIUS
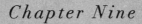

ANALECTS

A rule for advancement.

Reverent regard is due to youth. How are we to know
what they will be like in the future?

Yet, when they have reached the age of forty or fifty, if
they are still unknown in the world, then indeed they are
no longer worthy of such regard.

Discretion.

The Master said, "When I walk along with two others,
they may serve me as my teachers. I will select their good
qualities and follow them. I will observe their bad qualities
and avoid them."

The varieties of criticism.

Can anyone do otherwise than to assent to words said to them by way of correction? Let them reform themselves by such advice, and they will be reckoned valuable.

Can anyone be other than pleased with gentle words of persuasion? Let them comply fully with such words, and they will be accounted valuable.

With those who are pleased without complying, and those who assent but do not reform, I can do nothing.

The student's guide.

1. Give prominent place to loyalty and sincerity.
2. Associate only with those who are at a level comparable to your own.
3. When you have erred, do not be afraid to correct yourself.

Seriousness.

The Master said:

"Learn as if you could not reach your object, and were always fearing also lest you should lose it."

The love of learning.

He, who from day to day recognizes what he does not yet have, and from month to month does not forget what he has attained to, may be said indeed to love to learn.

GAUTAMA BUDDHA

CONCENTRATION

The four trances.

And what, O priests, is the discipline in elevated concentration?

Whenever a priest, having isolated himself from sensual pleasures—having isolated himself from demeritorious traits, and still exercising reasoning, still exercising reflection—enters upon the first trance, which is produced by isolation and characterized by joy and happiness.

Then, through the subsidence of reasoning and reflection—and still retaining joy and happiness—he enters upon the second trance, which is an interior tranquilization and intentness of thoughts.

Then, through the paling of joy—indifferent, contemplative, conscious, and in the experience of bodily happiness, that state which eminent men describe when they say, "Indifferent, contemplative, and living happily"—he enters upon the third trance.

Then, through the abandonment of happiness—through the abandonment of misery, through the disappearance of all antecedent gladness and grief—he enters upon the fourth trance, which has neither misery nor happiness, but is contemplation as refined by indifference.

This, O priests, is called the discipline in elevated concentration.

What advantage, O priests, is gained by training in quiescence?

The thoughts are trained.

And what advantage is gained by the training of the thoughts?

Passion is abandoned.

HUI HAI

ILLUMINATION

Release from time in the pursuit of freedom.

So long as your mind is fixed solely on the void, there is nothing to which you can attach yourself.

If you want to understand the unattached mind clearly, while you are actually sitting in meditation you must be cognizant only of the mind and not permit yourself to make judgments. You must avoid evaluations in terms of good, evil, or anything else. Whatever is past is past, so do not sit in judgment upon it. When minding about the past ceases of itself, it can be said that there is no longer any past.

Whatever is in the future is not here yet, so do not direct your hopes and longings toward it. When minding about the future ceases of itself, it can be said that there is no future.

Whatever is present is now at hand. Just be conscious of your non-attachment to everything. Non-attachment is not allowing any love or aversion for anything to enter your mind. When minding the present ceases of itself, we may say that there is no present.

When there is no clinging to any of those three realities, they may be said not to exist.

Should your mind wander, do not follow it, whereupon your wandering mind will stop wandering of its own accord.

Should your mind desire to linger somewhere, do not follow it and do not dwell there, whereupon your mind's questing for a dwelling-place will cease of its own accord.

Thereby, you will come to possess a non-dwelling mind, a mind which remains in the state of non-dwelling. If you are fully aware in yourself of a non-dwelling mind, you will discover that there is just the fact of dwelling, with nothing to dwell upon or not to dwell upon.

This full awareness in yourself of a mind dwelling upon nothing is known as having a clear perception of your own mind and your own nature.

A mind which dwells upon nothing is the Buddha-Mind, the mind of one already delivered, Bodhi-Mind, Primal Mind.

It is also the realization that the nature of all appearances is unreal. It is this which the sutras call "patient realization of the Primal."

If you have not realized it yet, you must strive and strive, you must increase your exertions.

Then, when your efforts are crowned with success, you will have attained to understanding from within yourself, an understanding stemming from a mind that abides nowhere, by which we mean a mind free from delusion and reality alike.

A mind disturbed by love and aversion is deluded, a mind free from both is real.

A mind thus free reaches the state in which opposites are seen as void, whereby freedom and deliverance are obtained.

WANG YANG-MING

HOW TO MAKE PROGRESS IN KNOWLEDGE

The investigation of things: organic education and natural mind.

I made inquiry saying, "What shall the individual do when he finds that he is making no progress in knowledge?"

The Teacher said:

In devoting one's self to study, one must have a point of departure. One should work from the starting-point forward, and advance by gradually completing each branch of study.

The immortals have a good example when speaking of small children: "The child in its mother's womb consists only of pure vital force."

What knowledge can it have? After birth it is first able to cry; a little later, to laugh; still later, to recognize its parents and brothers; and after that it is able to stand, walk, grasp, and carry. This is universally true. It implies that mental and physical energy increases, that strength becomes more vigorous, and intelligence more ample as the days pass.

These capacities are not acquired through direct endeavor or through a series of investigations after birth.

Rather, there is a source.

That the sage, Confucius, assumed regal sway over Heaven and Earth, and nourished all things, is merely the result of progressive development from the equilibrium in which there is no stirring of pleasure, anger, sorrow, or joy.

Later scholars do not understand what is meant by "the investigation of things." They see that the sage was omniscient and omnipotent, and thereupon desire at the very beginning to complete their quest. Is that in harmony with natural law?

In fixing one's determination, one must work as though one were cultivating a tree.

When the young tree has the first rootlets, it does not yet have a trunk, and when the trunk appears, it does not yet have branches. After the branches come the leaves, and after the leaves, the flowers and the fruit.

When you first cultivate the roots, you need only care for them by watering them. You should not think of cultivating branches, leaves, flowers, and fruit. What advantage is there in being anxious? But you should not forget to care for the tree and water it, lest perchance there be no branches, leaves, flowers, or fruit.

I said: "What shall be done when one studies and is unable to understand?"

The Teacher said:

It shows that the quest is confined to the meaning of the individual words and characters, and that therefore one does not understand the thought of what is read.

This is not equal to the method of those who devoted themselves to education in ancient times, for they read much and were able to explain it. But the unfortunate thing was that, though they were able to expound very clearly, they did not really gain any advantage.

It is necessary to work from the base of native endowment.

Whosoever is unable to understand or unable to practice should return in his work to his original mind. Then he should be able to comprehend.

The Four Books and the Five Classics discuss the original nature of the mind.

The original nature of the mind is to be identified with the path of truth. He who understands the original nature of his mind thereby understands the path of truth, for the two cannot be separated.

This is the point of departure in studying.

Chapter Ten

ETHICS
AND
BEHAVIOR

WANG CHI

ON GOING TO A TAVERN

These days, continually fuddled with drink,
I fail to see the appetites of the soul.
But seeing men all behaving like drunkards,
How can I alone remain sober?

CONFUCIUS

ANALECTS

General ethical guidelines.

The Philosopher Tsang said:

I daily examine myself on three points:

Whether, in transacting business for others, I may not have been faithful.

Whether, in dealings with friends, I may not have been sincere.

Whether I may not have mastered and practiced the instructions of my teacher.

Principles of proper regard for one's fellows.

Yen Yuen asked about man's proper regard for his fellow-man.

The Master said to him, "Self-control, and a habit of falling back upon propriety effect it.

"Let these conditions be fulfilled for one day, and every one round will perform his duty. Is it to begin in oneself, do you think, or indeed, is it to begin in others?"

"Would you be good enough," said Yen Yuen, "to give me a summary of it?"

Then said the Master, "Unless you have propriety, do not use your eyes. Without it, do not use your ears, nor your tongue, nor a limb of your body."

"I hope I may not be lacking in diligence," said Yen Yuen, "and with your favor I will endeavor to carry out this advice."

Chung-kung also asked about man's proper regard for his fellows.

To him the Master replied thus: "When you go forth from your door, be as if you were meeting some guest of importance.

"When you are dealing with the common people, be as if you were taking part in a great religious function.

"Do not set before others what you do not desire yourself.

"Let there be no resentful feelings against you when you are away in the country, and none when at home."

"I hope I may not lack diligence," said Chung-kung, "but with your favor I will endeavor to carry out this advice."

Sz-ma Niu asked the same question.

The answer he received was this: "The words of the man who has a proper regard for his fellows are uttered with difficulty."

"His words are uttered with difficulty?" he echoed in surprise. "What has this to do with proper regard for one's fellow-creatures?"

"Where there is difficulty in *doing*," the Master replied, "will there not be some difficulty in *utterance*?"

The same disciple asked a question about the superior man.

"Superior men," the Master replied, "are free from trouble and apprehension."

"Free from trouble and apprehension?" said Sz-ma Niu. "How does that make them superior men?"

The Master added, "Where there is found, upon introspection, to be no chronic disease, how shall there be any trouble? How shall there be any apprehension?"

The same disciple, being troubled, remarked, "I am alone in having no brother, while all others have theirs—younger or elder."

The Master said to him, "I have heard this: 'Death and life have destined times; wealth and honors rest with Heaven. Let the superior man keep watch over himself without ceasing, showing deference to others—with propriety of manners—and all within the four seas will be his brethren. How should he be distressed for lack of brothers!'"

Dispensing with illusory virtue.

Fan Ch'i, strolling with the Master over the ground below the place of the rain-dance, said to him, "I venture to ask how to raise the standard of virtue, how to reform dissolute habits, and how to discern what is illusory."

"Ah! a good question indeed!" exclaimed the Master. "Is not putting duty first and success second a way of raising the standard of virtue? And is not attacking the evil in oneself, rather than the evil which is in others, a way of reforming dissolute habits? And as to illusions—is not one morning's fit of anger, causing a man to forget himself, and even involving in the consequences those who are near and dear to him—is not that an illusion?"

Guiding one who has gone astray.

Tze-kung was consulting the Master about a friend.

"Speak to him frankly and respectfully," said the Master, "and gently lead him on.

"If you do not succeed, then stop. Do not submit yourself to indignity."

OTHER SAYINGS OF THE MASTER

Meditations on the superior and the common.

When the superior man regards righteousness as the essential thing, gives operation to it according to the rules of propriety, lets it issue in humility and become complete in faithfulness—there indeed is your superior man.

The problem of the superior man will be his own want of ability.

It will be no problem to him that others do not know him.

The superior man is exacting of himself.

The common man is exacting of others.

A superior man has self-respect, and he does not strive. He is sociable, yet belongs to no party.

He does not promote a man because of his words, nor does he pass over the words because of the man.

The faults of the superior man are like the eclipses of the sun and moon.

He has his faults, and all men see them.

He changes again, and all men look up to him.

———

What is disliked by the masses needs inquiring into; also does that which they have a preference for.

———

Not to retract after committing an error may itself be called error.

———

The superior man has nine things which are subjects with him of thoughtful consideration.

In regard to the use of his eyes, he is anxious to see clearly.

In regard to the use of his ears, he is anxious to hear distinctly.

In regard to his countenance, he is anxious that it should be benign.

In regard to his demeanor, he is anxious that it should be respectful.

In regard to his speech, he is anxious that it should be sincere and truthful.

In regard to his doing of business, he is anxious that it should be reverently careful.

In regard to what he doubts about, he is anxious to question others.

When he is angry, he thinks of the difficulties that come from anger.

When he sees gain to be had, he thinks of righteousness.

Rules of behavior.

Confucius, in his village, looked simple and sincere, as if he were not able to speak.

When he was in the prince's ancestral temple, or in the court, he spoke minutely on every point, but cautiously.

When he was waiting at court, in speaking with the great officers of the lower grade, he spoke freely, but in a direct manner.

In speaking with those of the higher grade, he did so blandly, but precisely.

When the ruler was present, his manner displayed respectful uneasiness; it was grave, but self-possessed.

When the prince called him to employ him in the reception of a visitor, his countenance appeared to change, and his legs to move forward with difficulty.

He inclined himself to the other officers among whom he stood, moving his left or right arm, as their position required, but keeping the skirts of his robe before and behind evenly adjusted. He hastened forward, with his arms like the wings of a bird. When the guest had retired, he would report to the prince, "The visitor is not turning around any more."

When he entered the palace gate, he seemed to bend his body, as if the gate were not sufficient to admit him.

When he was standing, he did not occupy the middle of the gateway.

When he passed in or out, he did not tread upon the threshold.

When he was passing the vacant place of the prince, his countenance appeared to change, and his legs to bend under him, and his words came as if he hardly had the breath to utter them.

He ascended the reception hall, holding up his robe with both his hands, and his body bent; holding in his breath also, as if he dared not breathe.

When he came out from the audience, as soon as he had descended one step, he began to relax his countenance, and had a satisfied look. When he had got to the bottom of the steps, he advanced rapidly to his place, with his arms like wings, and on occupying it, his manner still showed respectful uneasiness.

When he was carrying the scepter of his ruler, he seemed to bend his body, as if he were not able to bear its weight. He did not hold it higher than the position of the hands in making a bow, nor lower than their position in giving anything to another.

His countenance seemed to change, and look apprehensive, and he dragged his feet along as if they were held by something to the ground.

In presenting the presents with which he was charged, he wore a placid appearance.

At his private audience, he looked highly pleased.

Reciprocity.

Tze-kung asked, "Is there one word which may serve as a rule of practice for all one's life?"

The Master said, "Is not reciprocity such a word? What you do not want done to yourself, do not do to others."

Care in speech.

For one word a man is often deemed to be wise, and for one word he is often deemed to be foolish.

We ought to be careful indeed in what we say.

DOCTRINE OF THE MEAN

In favor of hidden virtue.

It is said in the *Book of Poetry*, "Over her embroidered robe she puts a plain, single garment," intimating a dislike for the display of the elegance of the former.

Just so, it is the way of the superior man to prefer the concealment of his virtue, while it daily becomes more illustrious, and it is the way of the lesser man to seek notoriety, while he daily goes more and more to ruin.

It is characteristic of the superior man to appear insipid, yet never to outstay his welcome; to show a simple negligence, yet to have his accomplishments recognized; to seem plain, yet to be discriminating.

He knows how what is distant lies in what is near. He knows where the wind proceeds from. He knows how what is minute becomes manifested. Such a one, we may be sure, will enter into virtue.

MO TZU

ON ALL-EMBRACING LOVE

A simple solution for the world's ills.

The sage man who takes in hand the ordering of society must know what it is that gives rise to disorder.

Only then can he put it in order.

If he does not know what gives rise to disorder, then he cannot make order. This is illustrated by the physician and his battle against disease. He must know what it is that gives rise to disease. Only so can he do battle.

Thus the sage man who is responsible for the ordering of society must examine what gives rise to disorder. When this examination is made, the rise of disorder is found to be people not loving each other, ministers of state and sons not being filial to their sovereigns and fathers.

That is what is called disorder. Sons love themselves and not their fathers, and the result is that they injure their fathers in profiting themselves. So in the case of fathers who have no compassion for their sons, and elder brothers for their younger brothers, and sovereigns for their ministers. This is universally described as disorder.

If we consider the robbers all over the country, it is just the same. Robbers love their households and do not love the households of others. The result is that they rob these other households in order to profit their own.

The same applies to the great officers who throw each other's clans into confusion and the feudal lords who attack each other's countries.

Examine all this as to its origin. It all comes from failure to love one another. If the whole of society had mutual love without discrimination, country would not attack country, clan would not throw clan into confusion. There would be no robbers. Sovereigns and ministers, fathers and sons, all would be compassionate and filial. In this state of affairs it follows that the Great Society would be well ordered.

Thus it was that our Master Mo said that he could not but urge that men should be loved. This is his word.

The knights and gentlemen everywhere today, however, say that although in theory this kind of all-embracingness is very good, nonetheless it is very difficult for universal application.

The profitability of love.

The word of our Master Mo is:

The leaders in society simply do not understand what is to their profit, nor do they distinguish the facts.

Take the example of a city under siege.

To fight in the fields, and so to achieve fame at the cost of one's life, this is what all men everywhere find very difficult. Yet if their sovereign calls for it, then the whole body of knights are able to do it.

How very different from this is mutual all-embracing love and the mutual exchange of profit. To love and benefit another is to have him love and benefit you. To hate and injure another is to have him hate and injure you.

What is there difficult in this? The fact is simply that no ruler has embodied it in his government and no knight has embodied it in his conduct.

The practicability of love.

Formerly Duke Ling of Ch'u State liked his knights to have small waists. Thus it was that his court officers all limited themselves to one meal a day. Having exhaled their breath, they tightened their belts. It was only by leaning against a wall that they could stand up. Within a year the whole court was black in the face. There is the fact: The sovereign called for it, and the ministers were able to do it. This is the kind of thing which people find to be difficult.

Nonetheless, the knights and gentlemen everywhere say that all-embracing love cannot be put into practice. To illustrate this they say it would be like picking up Mount T'ai and stepping over the river Ch'i.

The word of our Master Mo denounces this as an illustration. He said that picking up Mount T'ai and stepping over the river Ch'i should be described as beyond the limit of human strength, and from antiquity down to the present day there never has been a man who could do this. How different is mutual all-embracing love and the mutual exchange of benefits.

In the old days the Sage-kings put it into practice.

How is it known that this was so? In the old days when Yu brought society into order, he dug out the West River and Yu Tou River in order to drain off the waters of the Ch'u, Sun, and Huang Rivers. In the north he dammed the Yuan and Ku Rivers in order to fill up the Hou Chih Ti and Hu Chih basins. He made a watershed of the Ti Chu range and made a tunnel through Mount Nung Men. He did this to benefit the people of the Yui, Tai, Hu, and Ho tribes together with the people west of the Yellow River. This expresses what Yu did.

I, today, can practice all-embracingness.

Our Master Mo said that the man who criticizes others must have something as an alternative. To criticize without an alternative is like using fire to put out a fire. The idea the man expresses is logically indefensible.

I regard all-embracingness as exactly right. In this way quick ears and clear eyes cooperate in hearing and seeing, arms and legs are immeasurably strengthened to cooperate in movement and action, whilst those who possess the Way cooperate untiringly in teaching it.

In this way those who are old and without wife and child have their needs served so that they complete their tale of years, whilst the helpless young, children who are fatherless and motherless, have something they can trust so that their bodies can grow big and strong.

The advantages of mutual trust.

It is incomprehensible what it is that makes the knights on hearing about all-inclusiveness oppose it. What are the facts of the case?

As it is, the words of these knightly opponents do not stop at denunciation. They say, It is excellent, but nonetheless it is unusable.

The word of our Master Mo:

If it is unusable, even I will oppose it. How can it be both good and unusable? Let us go forward along two lines.

Suppose there are two knights, one of them holding fast to discrimination, the other to all-embracingness.

The one who discriminates will make the following statement: "It would be absurd for me to regard my friend's body as I regard my own, to regard his parents as I do my own." The result would be that when he observed his friend to be hungry and cold, he would not feed him or clothe him. When his friend was ill, he would not tend him. When his friend died, he would not bury him. These would be the words of the man who discriminates, and also his deeds.

The knight who is all-embracing would not speak or act in this manner.

He would say: "I have heard that the high-minded knight must regard his friend's body as his own, his friend's parents as his own, and only then can he be regarded as a high-minded knight." The result would be that when he observed his friend to be hungry and cold, he would feed and clothe him.

Now if we understand that the words of the two knights contradict each other and their actions are diametrically opposed, we have to assume that both speak the truth and both act accordingly, so that each man's words and actions agree like the two halves of a tally. Not a word is spoken which is not put into practice.

In that case the question may well be put:

Suppose a man puts on his harness for going out on a campaign in which the scale of life and death cannot be known. Do you know to whom he would entrust his household and his parents and the care of his wife and children?

Would it be to the friend who was all-embracing or the friend who discriminated?

I think that on such an occasion as this there are no fools anywhere, whether men or women.

Even though he were opposed to the all-embracing man, he would still put him in charge.

LAO TZU

Tao Te Ching

Ethical paradoxes.

My words are very easy to understand,
And very easy to practice;
But there is no one in the world who is able to under-
stand and to practice them.

There is an originating and all-comprehending
*   principle in my words,*
And an authoritative law.
Because they do not understand this,
Men do not know me.
They who know me are few,
And those who do not know me are honored.
It is thus that the sage wears rough garments,
While he carries the jade in his heart.

CHUANG TZU

Death and mourning.

When Lao Tan died, Khin Shih went to condole with his son, but after crying out three times, he came out.

The disciples said to him, "Were you not a friend of the Master?"

"I was," he replied.

And they said, "Is it proper then to offer your condolences merely as you have done?"

He said, "It is. At first I thought he was the man of men, and now I do not think so. When I entered a little ago and expressed my condolences, there were the old men wailing as if they had lost a son, and the young men wailing as if they had lost their mother.

"In his attracting and uniting them to himself in such a way, there must have been that which made them involuntarily express their words of condolence, and involuntarily wail, as they were doing.

"And this quality of his, which attracted and united in this fashion, was a hiding from himself of his Heavenly nature, and an excessive indulgence of his feelings. It was a forgetting of what he had received in being born; what the ancients called the punishment due to neglecting the Heavenly nature.

"When the Master came, it was at the proper time. When he went away, it was the simple consequence of his coming.

"Quiet acquiescence in what happens at its proper time, and quietly submitting to its ceasing afford no occasion for grief or for joy.

"The ancients described death as the loosening of the cord on which God suspended life. What we can point to are the ashes that have been consumed; but the fire is transmitted elsewhere, and we know not that it is over and ended."

LU HSIANG-SHAN

LAW, MIND, AND NATURE

Meditations on unity and universality.

Po-min asked: "How is one to investigate things?"

The Teacher, Lu Hsiang-shan, said: "Investigate the Law of things."

Po-min said, "The ten thousand things under Heaven are extremely multitudinous; how, then, can we investigate all of them exhaustively?"

The Teacher replied:

"The ten thousand things are already complete in us. It is only necessary to apprehend their Law. This Law fills the universe. Even Heaven and Earth, even ghosts and spirits, cannot diverge from it. How much less, then, can men?

"If one genuinely understands this Law, there can be no partiality between another person and myself. The good which others possess is a good that I also possess.

"To investigate things is to investigate this Law.

"Fu Hsi looked up to contemplate the brilliant forms exhibited in Heaven, and looked down to survey the patterns shown on Earth. He was, indeed, the first to exert his effort in thus apprehending this Law. If it were not so, what is called the investigation of things would be an insignificant matter.

"Fundamentally, this is what Heaven has bestowed upon us, and it is not imposed on us from without. To comprehend this Law is to become lord over oneself. He who can truly thus become lord cannot then be moved by external things, or influenced by depraved talk.

"What troubles you, my friend, is precisely that you do not apprehend this Law, are not lord over yourself, and have already become entangled in superficial doctrines and empty theories. All day long you rely only on external opinions to be your 'master,' whereas what Heaven has bestowed you make your 'guest.'

"Thus the positions of master and guest are reversed.

"You are led astray, thus being unable to return, and are deceived, thus being unable to gain a clarification. Simple and clear is this Law, so that it may be understood by women and children when they hear it. And yet pédants become lost and deceived. They create for themselves irrelevant theories, in which they wrap themselves.

"The ten thousand things are profusely contained within the square inch of space that is the Mind. Filling the Mind, and by pouring forth, filling the entire universe, there is nothing that is not this Law.

"It is extremely difficult for man to learn. All things which are covered by Heaven, supported by Earth, born in spring, grown in summer, reaped in autumn, and stored in winter, are embodied in this Law. Man, who lives in the midst of them, must keenly understand this Law and know how to explain it.

"The extensiveness of the knowledge of the Superior Man of ancient times has been highly esteemed. And yet to know exhaustively all the things under Heaven means nothing more than to know this Law. To have an extensive and wide view means to attach value to fine subtleties. Knowledge or non-knowledge fundamentally adds or subtracts nothing from this Law.

"How can this Law not exist in us? If we make our Will firm and unwavering, then this Law will daily become clearer and brighter, like a stream which daily grows more luxuriant.

"The Law which I apprehend is the correct, real, eternal, and universal Law of the world.

"This is the meaning of the passage. 'The Way is rooted in his own person, and sufficient attestation of it is given by the masses of the people. He examines it by comparison with that of the Three Kings, and finds it without mistake. He sets it up before Heaven and Earth, and there is nothing in it that is contradictory. He presents himself with it before ghosts and spirits, and no doubts about it arise. He is prepared to wait for the appearance of a sage a hundred ages after, and has no misgivings.

"Scholars truly must exhaust this Law, and apprehend this Law.

"Beyond the Way nothing exists; outside of things, there is no Way.

"The true Law under Heaven does not admit of duality. If one apprehends this Law, one will find that Heaven and Earth cannot differ from it, the sages and worthies of a thousand ages cannot differ from it.

"In every kind of business, one should only observe what the Law is, rather than being concerned with who the man in the business is.

"Men are not trees or stones; how, then, can they be without Mind? It is the noblest and the greatest among the five senses.

"The things that lie within the universe are those that lie within myself; the things that lie within myself are those that lie within the universe. Thus, the universe is my Mind and my Mind is the universe.

"If in the Eastern Sea there were to appear a sage, he would have this same Mind and this same Law. If in the Western Sea there were to appear a sage, he would have this same Mind and this same Law. If in the Southern or Northern Seas there were to appear sages, they too would have this same Mind and this same Law. If a hundred or a thousand generations ago, or a hundred or a thousand generations hence sages were to appear, they likewise would have this same Mind and this same Law.

"All men have this Mind, and all Minds are endowed with Law. Hence, Mind is the same as Law.

"It is therefore said: 'Law and Righteousness are agreeable to the Mind, just as the flesh of grass and grain-fed animals is agreeable to my mouth. What is to be valued in the scholar is his desire to plumb to the utmost this Law and to develop completely this Mind.

"If the sages and worthies of a thousand ages of antiquity were to be assembled at the same table, there would certainly be no Law on which they would be wholly in agreement. And yet this Mind and this Law are one in principle throughout ten thousand ages.

"In all affairs and all things under Heaven there is only one Law, there are not two Laws.

"Law is the universal Law of all under Heaven. Mind is the common Mind of all under Heaven.

"Mind is one Mind, and Law is one Law. Oneness pertains to them throughout, and even in their most subtle meaning they contain no duality. This Mind and this Law truly do not admit of any dualism.

"Mankind has been allotted an intermediate position between Heaven and Earth in which to live. Holding this favored position, there are no men whose Original Minds are not good.

"The four fundamental principles are all innately possessed by men; they are complete without any increase being made to them.

"Our Original Mind is not imposed on us from without. In its original state, is it not peaceful and harmonious, and, furthermore, without impediment? If we do not follow it with care and guard over it with stern attention, wicked influences and bad habits may take advantage of our negligence to assault us, and will thus destroy our Original Mind.

"Human Nature is originally good. Any evil in it results from the changes made upon it by external things. He who knows the injury caused by those external things, and who can revert to himself, can then know that goodness is the innate possession of our Nature.

"Where there is good there must be evil. The transition from one to the other is truly the turning over of one's hand. Goodness, however, is so from the very beginning, whereas evil comes into existence only as a result of turning over.

"What is it that will injure your Mind? It is Desire. When Desires are many, what we can preserve of our Original Mind is inevitably little; and when Desires are few, what we can preserve of our Original Mind is inevitably much.

"Therefore, the Superior Man does not worry that his Mind is not preserved, but rather worries that his Desires are not made few. For if the Desires were eliminated, the Mind would automatically be preserved. Thus, then, does not the preserving of what is good in our Mind depend upon the elimination of what does it injury?

"Common men are submerged by poverty or wealth, or by high or low position, or by benefit or injury, or by profit or loss, or by sounds and colors, or by sensuality and Desire. They destroy their virtuous Mind, and have no regard for Righteousness and Law. How very lamentable it is!

"Those who follow Material Desires gallop without knowing where to stop. Those who follow opinions also gallop without knowing where to stop. Therefore, although the Way is near, yet they seek for it afar; although a thing is easy, yet they seek for it in difficulty.

"But is the Way really remote or the thing difficult? Their opinions are unsound, that they make difficulties for themselves. If one fully realizes one's error, then one's doubts will be dissipated and one will reach the place in which to stop.

"The Way fills the universe, nowhere being concealed. It is, in Heaven, called the Negative [yin] and Positive [yang] principles. In Earth it is called Softness and Hardness. And in man it is called Humanity and Righteousness.

"The foolish and unworthy, being deficient, are blinded by Material Desire, and thus lose their Original Mind. Whereas the worthy and intelligent, going too far, are also blinded by their superficial views.

"The foolish and unworthy, being deficient, have never attained the Mean; the worthy and intelligent, going too far, have likewise never attained the Mean. Having a weakness for luxuries, they become accustomed to cunning and evil doings, become fettered by trivial and insignificant matters, and fall to high-sounding theories and superficial doctrines.

"They who lived in the prosperous, well-governed days of old, and who enjoyed the favor of the early Sage-kings, were surely without this fault. But now, because they live in later generations, when the doctrines of the early sages have been interrupted, when the Way has been destroyed, and when strange theories and depraved doctrines expand and spread, even resolute scholars come to grief and disaster. Thus they, as well as those ordinary men of the world who give rein to their Passions and indulge their Desires, all are drowned."

WANG YANG-MING

PRACTICAL ETHICAL INSTRUCTION

Self-mastery.

The Teacher said:

"Seize hold of a good resolution as if the mind were distressed. Will there be any time to engage in idle talk or to care for idle affairs, if the mind is fully occupied with its distress?"

I, Lu Ch'eng, made inquiry saying, "There is the matter of mastering one's mind. If in studying, one is engaged entirely with study, or in receiving guests, one is completely engaged in receiving guests, may these be considered as examples of being undivided?"

The Teacher said: "If in being fond of women one gives one's self completely to salaciousness, or if in desiring wealth one devotes one's self entirely to covetousness, may these be considered as instances of mastering one's mind? This is what is called submitting to urges, and should not be considered as mastering the mind. To master one's mind implies mastering moral principles."

Chapter Eleven

QUALITY
AND
PRODUCTIVITY

CONFUCIUS

ANALECTS

Accuracy before force.

The Master said:

In archery it is not going through the leather which is the principal thing—because people's strength is not equal.

This was the old way.

The big picture takes precedence over speed and detail.

Tze-hsia, being governor of Chu-fu, asked about government.

The Master said,

"Do not be desirous to have things done quickly.

"Do not look at small advantages.

"Desire to have things done quickly prevents their being done thoroughly. Looking at small advantages prevents great affairs from being accomplished."

LAO TZU

TAO TE CHING

The patterns and aesthetics of opposites.
    All in the world know beauty when they see it,
    And this is only because there is ugliness.
    They all know good at first sight,
    And this is only because there is evil.
    So it is that existence and non-existence are created
        one from the other;
    That difficulty and ease are produced one from the
        other;
    That long and short are fashioned one out of the figure
        of the other;
    That high and low arise from the contrast of one with
        the other;
    That the musical notes and tones become harmonious
        through the relation of one with another;
    And that front and back give the idea of one following
        another.

*Therefore the sage manages affairs without doing
     anything,*
And conveys his instructions without the use of speech.
All things spring up and are manifest.
*They grow, and there is no claim made for their
     ownership;*
*They go through their processes, and there is no
     expectation.*
The work is accomplished, and then it is forgotten.
In this way, it lasts forever.

————

It is the way of the Tao to act without acting;
To conduct business without doing anything;
To taste without discerning any flavor;
To magnify the small;
To multiply the few;
To reward injury with kindness.
*The master anticipates things that are difficult while
     they are still easy,*
And achieves greatness in small things.
All difficult things in the world
*Are sure to arise from a previous state in which they
     were easy,*
And all great deeds arise from small acts.
Therefore the sage, while he never does what is great,
Is able on that account to accomplish the greatest things.

He who lightly promises is sure to keep little faith.
He who thinks things easy is sure to find them difficult.
Therefore the sage sees difficulty even in what seems easy,
And so never has any difficulties.

The Way of production.
All things are produced by the Tao,
And nourished by its goodness.
They receive their forms according to the nature of each,
And are shaped according to their circumstances.
Therefore all things without exception honor the Tao,
And exalt its goodness.
This honoring of the Tao and exalting of its operation
Are always a spontaneous tribute.
Thus it is that the Tao produces all things,
Nourishes them by its goodness,
Brings them to their full growth,
Nurses them, completes them,
Matures them, maintains them, and overspreads them.
It produces them and makes no claim to possess them.
It carries them through their processes and does not
*   take credit.*
It brings them to maturity and exercises no control
*   over them.*
This is called primal good.

MO TZU

ON STANDARD PATTERNS

The need for standards, and an exposition of their ultimate source.

Anyone who takes any business in hand cannot dispense with a standard pattern.

If there is no standard, the business cannot succeed.

Even the best experts who act as generals and counselors-of-state all have standards for action. So also even with the best craftsmen. They use a carpenter's square for making squares and compasses for making circles, a piece of string for making straight lines and a plumb line for getting the perpendicular. It makes no difference whether a craftsman is skilled or not. All alike use these five devices as standards. Only the skilled are accurate. But, although the unskilled fail to be accurate, they nevertheless get much better results if they follow these standards in the work they do. Thus it is that craftsmen in their work have the measurements which these standards give.

Now take the great ones who rule our society, and the less great ones who rule the different states, but who have no standards of measurement for their actions.

In this they are less critically minded than the craftsman. That being so, what standard may be taken as suitable for ruling?

Will it do if everybody imitates his father and mother? The number of fathers and mothers is large, but the number of humane ones is small. If everybody were to imitate his father and mother, this standard would not be a humane one. For a standard to be not humane makes it impossible for it to be a standard.

Will it do then if everybody imitates his teacher? The number of teachers is large, but the number of humane ones is small. If everybody were to imitate his teacher, this standard would not be a humane one.

Will it do then if everybody imitates his sovereign? The number of princes is large, but the number of humane ones is small. If everybody imitated his sovereign, this standard would not be a humane one. Hence, fathers and mothers, teachers and sovereigns cannot be taken as standards for ruling.

All this being so, what standard may be taken as suitable for ruling?

The answer is that nothing is equal to imitating Heaven.

Heaven's actions are all-inclusive and not private-minded. Heaven's blessings are substantial and unceasing, its revelations abiding and incorruptible. Thus it was that the Sage-kings imitated it. Having taken Heaven as their standard, their every movement and every action was bound to be measured in relation to Heaven. What Heaven wanted, that they did. What Heaven did not want, that they stopped doing.

The question now is, what does Heaven want and what does it not want? Heaven wants men to love and be profitable to each other, and does not want men to hate and maltreat each other.

How do we know that Heaven wants men to love and be profitable to each other? Because it embraces all in its love of them, embraces all in its benefits to them. How do we know that Heaven embraces all? Because it embraces all in its possession of them and in its gifts of food.

I say that Heaven is sure to give happiness to those who love and benefit other men, and is sure to bring calamities on those who hate and maltreat other men.

CHUANG TZU

Skill and art.

His cook was cutting up an ox for the ruler Wan-hui. Whenever he applied his hand, leaned forward with his shoulder, planted his foot, and employed the pressure of his knee, in the audible ripping off of the skin, and slicing operation of the knife, the sounds were all in regular cadence.

The ruler said, "Ah! Admirable! That your art should have become so perfect!"

Having finished his operation, the cook laid down his knife, and replied, "What your servant loves is the method of the Tao, something in advance of any art. When I first began to cut up oxen, I saw nothing but the entire carcass. After three years I ceased to see it as a whole. Now I deal with it in a spiritlike manner, and do not look at it with my eyes. The use of my senses is discarded, and my spirit acts as it wills. Observing the natural lines, my knife slips through the great crevices and slides through the great cavities, taking advantage of the facilities thus presented. My art avoids the membranous ligatures, and much more the great bones.

"A good cook changes his knife every year; it may have been injured in cutting. An ordinary cook changes his every month; it may have been broken.

"Now my knife has been in use for nineteen years; it has cut up several thousand oxen, and yet its edge is as sharp as if it had newly come from the whetstone. When applied to the interstices of the joints, the edge of the knife has no appreciable thickness. How easily it moves along! The blade has more than enough room.

"Nevertheless, whenever I come to a complicated joint, and see that there will be some difficulty, I proceed anxiously and with caution, not allowing my eyes to wander from the place, and moving my hand slowly. Then by a very slight movement of the knife, the part is quickly separated, and drops like earth to the ground. Then standing up with the knife in my hand, I look all round, and in a leisurely manner, with an air of satisfaction, wipe it clean, and put it in its sheath."

The ruler Wan-hui said, "Excellent! I have heard the words of my cook, and learned from them the nourishment of life."

Nature subverted by art and government.

Horses can with their hoofs tread on the hoarfrost and snow, and with their hair withstand the wind and cold; they feed on the grass and drink water; they prance with their legs and leap—this is the true nature of horses. Though there were made for them grand towers and large dormitories, they would prefer not to use them.

But when Po-lao, the first tamer, said, "I know well how to manage horses," men proceeded to singe and mark them, to clip their hair, to pare their hoofs, to halter their heads, to bridle them and hobble them, and to confine them in stables and corrals. When subjected to this treatment, two or three in every ten of them died.

Men proceeded further to subject horses to hunger and thirst, to gallop them and race them, and to make them go together in regular order. In front were the evils of the bit and ornamented breastbands, and behind were the terrors of the whip and switch. When so treated, more than half of them died.

The first potter said, "I know well how to deal with clay," and men proceeded to mold it into circles as exact as if made by the compass, and into squares as exact as if formed by the measuring square.

The first carpenter said, "I know well how to deal with wood," and men proceeded to make it bent as a hook, and straight as a plumb line.

But is it the nature of clay and wood to require the application of the compass and square, of the hook and line?

And yet age after age men have praised Po-lao, saying, "He knew well how to manage horses," and also the first potter and carpenter, saying, "They knew well how to deal with clay and wood."

This is just the error committed by the governors of the world.

According to my idea, those who know well how to govern mankind should not act so.

The people had their regular and constant nature. They wove and made themselves clothes; they tilled the ground and got food. This was their common faculty. They were all one in this, and did not form themselves into separate classes; so were they constituted and left to their natural tendencies.

Therefore in the age of perfect virtue men walked along with slow and grave step, and with their looks steadily directed forward.

At that time, on the hills there were no footpaths, nor excavated passages; on the lakes there were no boats nor dams; all creatures lived in companies; and the places of their settlement were made close to one another. Birds and beasts multiplied to flocks and herds; the grass and trees grew luxuriant and long. In this condition the birds and beasts might be led about without feeling the constraint; the nest of the magpie might be climbed to, and peeped into. Yes, in the age of perfect virtue, men lived in common with birds and beasts, and were on terms of equality with all creatures, as forming one family. How could they know among themselves the distinctions of superior men and small men?

Equally without knowledge, men did not leave the path of their natural virtue. Equally free from desires, they were in the state of pure simplicity. In that state of pure simplicity, the nature of the people was what it ought to be.

But when the sagely men appeared, limping and wheeling about in the exercise of benevolence, pressing along and standing on tiptoe in the doing of righteousness, then men universally began to be perplexed.

Those sages also went to excess in their performances of music, and in their gesticulations in the practice of ceremonies, and then men began to be separated from one another.

If the raw materials had not been cut and hacked, who could have made a sacrificial vase from them?

If the natural jade had not been broken and injured, who could have made the handles for the libation cups from it?

If the attributes of the Tao had not been disallowed, how should they have preferred benevolence and righteousness?

If the instincts of the nature had not been departed from, how should ceremonies and music have come into use?

If the five colors had not been confused, how should the ornamental figures have been formed?

If the five notes had not been confused, how should they have supplemented them by the musical accords?

The cutting and hacking of the raw materials to form vessels was the crime of the skillful workman.

The injury done to the characteristics of the Tao in order to practice benevolence and righteousness was the error of the sagely men.

Natural talent. The parable of the swimmer.

Confucius was looking at the cataract near the gorge of Lu, which fell a height of 240 cubits, and the spray of which floated a distance of forty miles, producing a turbulence in which no tortoise, crocodile, fish, or turtle could play.

He saw, however, an old man swimming about in it, as if he had sustained some great calamity, and wished to end his life.

Confucius made his disciples hasten along the stream to rescue the man; but by the time they had gone several hundred paces, he was walking along singing, with his hair disheveled, and enjoying himself at the foot of the embankment.

Confucius followed and asked him, saying, "I thought you were a sprite; but, when I look closely at you, I see that you are a man. Let me ask if you have any particular way of treading the water."

The man said, "No, I have no particular way. I began to learn the art at the very earliest time. As I grew up, it became my nature to practice it, and my success in it is now as sure as fate. I enter and go down with the water in the very center of its whirl, and come up again with it when it whirls the other way. I follow the way of the water, and do nothing contrary to it of myself. This is how I tread it."

Confucius said, "What do you mean by saying that your success in it now is as sure as fate?"

The man replied, "I was born among these hills and lived contented among them. That is why I say that I have trod this water from my earliest time. I grew up by it, and have been happy treading it. That is why I said that to tread it had become natural to me. I know not how I do it, and yet I do it. That is why I say that my success is as sure as fate."

A sense of fitness.

To be unthought of by the foot that wears it is the fitness of a shoe.

To be unthought of by the waist is the fitness of a girdle.

When one's wisdom does not think of the right or the wrong of a matter, that shows the suitability of the mind for that matter.

When one is conscious of no inward change, or outward attraction, that shows the mastery of affairs.

He who perceives at once the fitness, and never loses the sense of it, has the fitness that forgets all about what is fitting.

.

The true workman.

The ruler Yuan of Sung wishing to have a map drawn, the masters of the pencil all came to undertake the task.

Having received his instructions and made their bows, they stood, licking their pencils and preparing their ink. Half their number, however, remained outside.

There was one who came late, with an air of indifference, and did not hurry forward. When he had received his instructions and made his bow, he did not keep standing, but proceeded to his shed. The duke sent a man to see him, and there he was, with his upper garment off, sitting cross-legged, and nearly naked.

The ruler said, "He is the man; he is a true draftsman."

HUAI-NAN TZU

PLACING CUSTOMS

Appreciating and utilizing nature's divergent forms.

Acting in one's Nature is called acting in the Way.

Attaining one's heavenly Nature is called attaining Virtue.

Only after the Nature is lost do we ennoble Altruism.

Only after the Way is lost do we ennoble Propriety.

Therefore, Altruism and Propriety being established, the Way and the Virtue will move away. If Rites and Music are adorned, then the pure and the Whole will be dispersed. If right and wrong take form, then the Hundred

Surnames will become bedazzled. If pearls and jade are honored, then all under heaven will compete.

All four of these are indeed products of deteriorating generations, usages of branch-tip generations.

Wide mansions and broad houses, vestibules in rows, and ante rooms which lead off in many directions are places in which a man is secure; a bird entering them becomes anxious.

High mountains and perilous precipices, deep woods and clumped brush are places in which the tiger and leopard take pleasure; a man entering them becomes fearful.

River valleys and pervasive moors, amassed waters and deep springs are places in which the turtle and lizard find advantage; a man entering them dies.

There are songs in which a man takes musical pleasure; a bird or beast hearing them is startled.

Deep gorges and sheer cliffs, prominent trees and high-stretching branches are places in which long-armed monkeys and long-tailed monkeys take pleasure; a man ascending them shudders.

The forms are distinctive, and the Natures are divergent. That which gives pleasure becomes that which gives grief. That which gives security becomes that which gives peril.

Then when we come to all that is covered and sustained by Heaven and Earth, and all that is shone upon and monitored by the sun and moon, let each be so deployed that it takes advantage within its Nature and is secure in its residence, and that it stays where it is fit to stay and performs within its abilities.

Truly, in the stupid there is an asset, and in the sagacious there is insufficiency.

A pillar may not be used to pick the teeth, and a hairpin may not be used to hold up a house.

A horse may not be used to pull what is heavy, and an ox may not be used to pursue what is swift.

Lead may not be used to make a sword, and bronze may not be used to make a crossbow.

Iron may not be used to make a boat, and wood may not be used to make a cooking pot.

We use each where it is best suited and apply it where it fits.

Clarity and peace in work.

One who does not hear the Way lacks means to revert to his Nature. Indeed, the Sage-kings of old were able to access the Way in the self, and their orders were put into practice, and their will was effected. Their fame was handed down to later generations, and their Virtue extended to the four seas.

Therefore, whenever one is about to undertake some business, one should first calm the mind and clear the spirit. If the spirit is clear and the mind calm, then matters may be corrected. It is like the impression of a seal put into clay. If the seal is placed correctly, the impression will be correct. If the seal is placed crookedly, the impression will be crooked.

The artisan as sage. The sage as artisan.

Thus, the sage man's shaping and preparing of things is somewhat like the hewing, trimming, drilling, and pegging of the carpenter, or the cutting, slicing, dividing, and separating of the butcher. The fit is obtained by bending, not by breaking or wounding.

If one is an inept craftsman, then this is not so. Big objects stop up the hole and will not go in, and small objects are too slender and do not fill the space around.

Now when the sage man hews and trims a thing, he cuts it and halves it, parts it and disperses it. Having taken license and having erred, he then plans a second attempt. He no sooner leaves its root than he returns to its gate. Having sculptured and having carved, once more he reverts to the original piece of wood. In his joining he acts within the Way and Virtue; in his parting he acts by the prevailing standards. In turning about he enters the somber mystery; in his dispersing he responds to the formless. Rites and propriety, moderation and practice—these can reach the trunk-root of perfect government.

The proper use of tools.

Indeed, even though engraving tool and gouge, trimmer and saw are laid out, if one is not a good craftsman, he will not be able to work the wood.

Even though furnace and bellows and earthen mold are set out, if one is not a skillful smith, he will not be able to govern the metal.

T'an, the butcher of oxen, dissected nine oxen in one morning, yet his knife still could be used to shave hair; and Ting, the kitchen-man, used his knife for nineteen years, yet the edge was as if it were newly made and whetstoned.

Why was this so?

They swam freely in the midst of the multitudinous voids.

It is like compass and square, hook and cord—these are the tools of skill, but they are not the means by which one becomes skillful.

Thus, with an unstringed zither, though one be the Music Master Wen, one cannot make a tune. If it is strung, one still may not be able to evoke sorrow. Truly, strings are the tools of sorrow, but they are not the means by which one evokes sorrow.

Now it is like the carpenter's connecting triggers, revolving openings, covert closures, and dizzy inlays. He enters into the minuteness of deep chaos and the extremity of spiritual concord. He swims freely amidst heart and hand, and there is no impinging on things.

A father is not able to instruct his son in this art.

The blind music master freed his mind to make manifest many things, and he copied spirits and excelled in dancing. This art took form in strings.

An elder brother is not able to explain this art to his younger brother.

Now then, the water level performs leveling, and the cord performs straightening. But it seems that their capacities do not lie within the cord and water level themselves.

How these tools may be used to level and straighten is a method which cannot be shared.

Truly, upon striking a note on one musical instrument, the corresponding string on a musical instrument close by will respond. These are the responses of the same sounds to each other.

Issues of relativity and fashion.

There are no grounds under Heaven upon which right and wrong can be fixed. Each generation takes as right that which is taken as right by it, and takes as wrong that which is taken as wrong by it. That which is called "right" and "wrong" by each generation is different.

All take themselves as right and take others as wrong.

Viewed in this light, things which suit the self still do not possess rightness at the outset, and those which oppose the heart still do not possess wrongness at the outset.

Truly, those who seek the right are not seeking the inner structure of the Way but are seeking to merge with the self. And those who push away the wrong do not smite the aberrant but push away an opposition to the heart.

But opposition to the ego does not mean that a thing cannot combine with other people, and combination with the ego does not mean that a thing is not in negation with custom.

The right of perfect rightness is without wrongness, and the wrong of perfect wrongness is without rightness. These are the true right and wrong.

Now it is like those who are right in this but wrong in that, wrong in this but right in that. This is called "one right, one wrong." This one right and wrong is only a nook and angle. That one right and wrong is space and time.

Now I wish to select the right and reside in it, and to select the wrong and push it away. Yet I do not know what is called right and wrong by this generation. I do not know which is right and which is wrong.

Advice in the face of modernity and transformation.

Truly, one who is merged with the Way is like a chariot wheel-axle. It does not revolve of itself, but it is carried along with the hub a thousand miles, turning about in the inexhaustible plains.

One who is not merged with the Way is like one meandering and in doubt. If he is given directions, he heeds those directions wherever he is, yet making one slight error he goes awry.

Suddenly he no longer has his bearings, and once again he is meandering and in doubt. Truly, he ends his life being menial to others. He is just like a vane when it feels the wind. Without a moment's hesitation, he is lost.

Thus, the sage man embodies the Way and reverts to his Nature. If one does not transform in anticipation of transformations, then one shall not succeed.

KUO HSIANG

CONTENTMENT

Living with limitation.

If a person is perfectly at ease with his spirit and physical power, whether he lifts something heavy or carries something light, it is due to the fact that he is using strength to a desired degree.

If a person loves fame and is not satisfied even when he has broken his back in the attempt, it is due to the fact that human knowledge knows no limit.

Therefore what is called knowledge is born of our losing our balance and will be eliminated when ultimate capacity is realized intuitively.

Intuitively realizing ultimate capacity means allowing one's lot to reach its highest degree, and, as in the case of lifting weights, not adding so much as an ounce beyond that.

Therefore though a person carries ten thousand pounds, if it is equal to his capacity he will surely forget the weight upon his body. Though a person attends to ten thousand matters, if his capacity is equal to them he will be utterly unaware that the matters are upon him. These are the fundamentals for the cultivation of life.

If one attains the Mean and intuitively realizes the proper limit, everything can be done. The cultivation of life does not seek to exceed one's lot but to preserve the principle of things and to live out one's allotted span of life.

Joy and sorrow are the results of gains and losses. A gentleman who profoundly penetrates all things and is in harmony with their transformations will be contented with whatever time may bring. He follows the course of nature in whatever situation he may be. He will be intuitively united with creation. He will be himself wherever he may be.

Where does gain or loss, life or death come in? Therefore, if one lets what he has received from nature take its own course, there will be no place for joy or sorrow.

Allow the foot to walk according to its capacity, and let the hand grasp according to its strength.

Listen to what the ear hears and see what the eye sees.

In knowing, stop at what cannot be known.

In action, stop at what cannot be done.

Employ the faculties as they would use themselves.

Do things that would be done by themselves.

Be unrestrained within one's lot but do not attempt the least thing outside of it.

This is the easiest way of taking no unnatural action. There has never been a case of taking no action and yet of one's nature and life not being preserved, and I have never heard of any principle according to which the preservation of nature and life is not a blessing.

The expert driver utilizes the natural capacity of horses to its limit.

To use the capacity to its limit lies in letting it take its own course. If forced to run at a rapid pace, with the expectation that they can exceed their capacity, horses will be unable to bear it and many will die.

On the other hand, if both worn-out and thoroughbred horses are allowed to use their proper strength and to adapt the pace to their given lot, even if they travel to the borders of the country, their nature will be fully preserved.

But there are those who, upon hearing the doctrine of allowing the nature of horses to take its own course, will say: "Then set the horses free and do not ride on them."

And there are those who, upon hearing the doctrine of taking no action, will immediately say: "It is better to lie down than to walk."

Why are they so much off the track and unable to return? In this they have missed Chuang Tzu's ideas to a very high degree.

If one is contented wherever one goes, one will be at ease wherever he may be. Even life and death cannot affect him, much less flood or fire.

The perfect man is not besieged by calamities, and this is not because he escapes from them but because he advances the principles of things and goes forward, and naturally comes into union with good fortune.

STEFAN RUDNICKI, was educated at Columbia University and the Yale School of Drama. First introduced to oriental studies at Columbia University, Mr. Rudnicki has spent thirty years exploring Eastern thought and applying ritual and non-linear narrative conventions to theater and film. Among his published books are five actors' resource texts, *Colin Powell and the American Dream*, which he co-authored with Judith Cummings, the award-winning adaption of Sun Tzu's *The Art of War*, and the novel *Wilde*.